KU-255-784

Social, Industrial and Environmental Studies

Alasdair Hogarth

Sociology Dept.
Univ of London
Goldsmiths' College
New Cross, SE14 6NW

Edward Arnold

© Alasdair Hogarth 1984

First published in Great Britain 1984
by Edward Arnold (Publishers) Ltd
41 Bedford Square
London WC1B 3DQ

Edward Arnold (Australia) Pty Ltd
80 Waverley Road, Caulfield East
Victoria 3145
Australia

Reprinted 1985

British Library Cataloguing in Publication Data

Hogarth, Alasdair
  Social, industrial and environmental studies.
  1. Great Britain—Social conditions—1945–
  I. Title
  941.085′8   HN385.5

ISBN 0-7131-0869-X

All rights reserved. No part of this publication may be reproduced, stored in a retrieval system, or transmitted in any form or by any means, electronic, photocopying, recording, or otherwise, without the prior permission of Edward Arnold (Publishers) Ltd.

Text set in 11/12pt Times Roman Compugraphic by Colset Private Ltd, Singapore.Printed and bound by Richard Clay (The Chaucer Press) Ltd, Bungay, Suffolk

Acknowledgements

The publishers would like to thank the following for permission to include copyright material:

Asda Stores; Barclays Bank plc; Just Desks; Kentish Ironcraft Ltd; John Lewis Partnership; The Littlewoods Organisation; the Lord Chancellor's Department; Montrose Products; the National Newspapers' Mail Order Protection Scheme; W H Smith & Son Limited and West Lothian District Council.

The Publishers wish to thank the following for their permission to use copyright illustrations:

Crown Copyright, Science Museum, London: pp 55, 58, 62, 631; Crown Copyright, COI: p 177; British Leyland: pp 3, 196b; Catherine Shakespeare Lane: p 12t; Curry Group plc: p 12b; F W Woolworth plc: p 13t; ASDA Stores: p 13b; British Petroleum Company plc: p 22; British Nuclear Fuels plc: p 32; Mansell Collection Ltd: p 45t; Metropolitan Police: p 47; Manchester Public Library: p 54; Edward Arnold: p 59; Ironbridge Gorge Museum: p 60; Science Museum, London: pp 61, 63r; English China Clays Group: p 65; John Twinning: pp 80, 93; Scottish New Towns: p 83; Diana Lanham: p 94t & b; Wimpey News: p 95; Midland Bank plc: p 98t; Abbey National: p 98b; Barnabys Picture Library: p 111; LINK/Orde Eliason: p 112; Harwell Environmental Safety Group: p 115; UN/Yutaka Nagata: p 189; Ferranti plc: pp 192, 193b; Mullard Limited: p 193t; Computer Games Ltd: p 194; Hewlett-Packard Ltd: p 196t; IBM UK Ltd: p 197; Seiko Time (UK) Ltd: p 198t; Texas Instruments: pp 198b, 199.

Contents

Foreword

This is a course book written for the social, industrial and environmental studies core of a variety of vocational preparation schemes in schools and colleges of further education. It will be particularly appropriate for CPVE schemes. It will also be useful for social and careers education schemes.

Some of the material contained in this book appears in *Understanding Industry* by Alasdair Hogarth, Arnold 1983.

1

Introduction

An industrial way of life

It is easy to think of a major disaster which would completely destroy the world as we know it. A nuclear war, perhaps, or the coming of another ice age; a plague killing millions of people, or a large asteroid from space crashing into our planet. Think what it would be like if you were one of the very few people left alive after such a catastrophe. There would be no towns or cities, no electricity or water supply. There would be no doctors, hospitals or schools; no factories, cars or television. You would have to grow or catch your own food, make your own clothes, collect your own water, and find ways of keeping yourself warm and sheltered. You would have to become *self-sufficient*.

This means you make everything you need on your own, or together with your family and a few friends, instead of being able to buy things from shops. But we do not need a disaster to find people living like this. In many parts of the world it is the normal way of life. Indeed, if we could go back in time we would not need to go very far to find the people in Britain living in a self-sufficient society.

It might sound rather attractive . . .

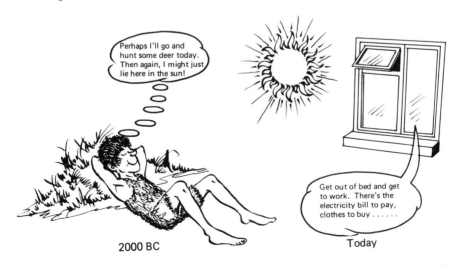

2000 BC

Today

In fact, that's not a fair comparison at all. Far from being a life of idleness, life in a primitive society is a life of back-breaking toil to get enough food to eat to fend off starvation. It is a never-ending battle against the weather, the winter, natural disasters, and sometimes wild animals. There is the constant fear of illness leading usually to death or disability. You would spend most of your time being hungry, cold and worried about the future.

By comparison, in Britain today we are surrounded by untold wealth. We may work for only eight hours a day, five days a week to provide ourselves not only with food, housing and clothes, but also holidays, cars, entertainments, luxuries and a vast number of devices to make life easier and more pleasant − like washing machines, showers, books and magazines, light, central heating, films and so forth.

What is wealth?

Our way of life is the benefit we get from living in an industrial society, where we have factories and machines producing enormous numbers of articles we would have no chance of making on our own: where large numbers of people can be completely freed from making things to provide services for everyone else − services like *health, education, the post office, hairdressing and public transport*.

The amount of goods and services a society produces is called the *wealth* of that society. A few other countries, like the United States, are wealthier than Britain, because they produce more goods and services, and therefore have more to share among their population. But most countries are a great deal less wealthy than we are. So much so, that many people in the world do not even have enough to eat, far less enjoy the wide range of goods and services we take for granted. Many people think it is unfair that a few countries have so much while the rest have so little, which is why some people in Britain give money to organizations like Oxfam, the Save the Children Fund, and UNICEF, to try and help those people in poorer countries. The government too, provides money and help to assist progress in the so-called 'under-developed' or developing nations.

How do we do it?

In this book we will be looking at how it happened that Britain became a wealthy, industrial society. We will be seeing how our industrial society works, and the part each one of us can play in preserving and increasing our wealth. We shall also be looking at the problems industry brings to us and to our environment, and what we can all do to help alleviate these problems.

We can start by getting one thing clear about manufacturing industry. (*Manufacturing* means making things in a factory with machines.) Some

British Leyland (Austin-Morris) factory, Cowley Division, Oxford

industry is dirty, smelly and noisy. Some industry pollutes our air, our sea, and our land and rivers. Working in some industries can be boring, hard and unpleasant. But above everything else, our industry is the foundation of our wealth: it supports our entire way of life, with all our goods and services. Without our industry to make the goods, and therefore provide the money for the services we depend on, we would find ourselves in a very different, and a much less pleasant, society.

Some questions to get you started

1   What is meant by the wealth of a society?

2   What does manufactured mean?

3   Make a list of the first *ten* manufactured goods you think of which you have used today. (You might start with your alarm clock!)

4   Now go through the list and *underline* those articles which you could have made yourself. It won't be many. For each of the others say why you couldn't have made it: was it because:
      You don't know how to?
      You know how to, but you don't have the machinery necessary?
      You don't know what it's made out of?
      All of these?

3

5   Electricity has only come into use during the present century. In this time we have come to rely on it enormously. List *six* items in your house which you regard as essential, yet which rely on electricity to make them work. How would you manage without them? Perhaps your house is built in such a way that you must have electricity?

6   Are there any major systems in your house that do not rely on electricity?

2

The firm

An industrial firm is like a magician's top hat — certain things go in, something happens to them, and they come out different. The magician waves a magic wand; the firm, unfortunately, has to do rather more! The things that go in are called the *raw materials*. These are the basic things the firm needs to make whatever it produces. The thing that comes out is called the *finished product* — this is what the firm is in business to produce, and what it sells to its customers.

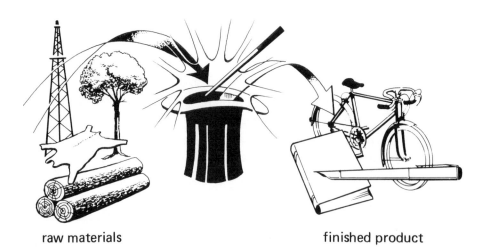

raw materials   finished product

Each finished product has one or more main raw materials, and a lot of more minor ones. For example, the main raw material for most shoes in leather, with various bits of metal, thread and rubber as minor raw materials. The main raw material for cars is steel, and so on.

Questions

1   What is a raw material?

2   The main raw material for cars is steel. List *five* other raw materials which also go into producing cars.

3   Take an item of clothing you are wearing which has a label on as your finished product. What have you chosen? Which firm produced this finished product? What were the firm's raw materials (it will say on the label).

Now read on

Every raw material started life originally as a natural product which was either grown or dug out of the ground. One firm after another will have done something to this natural product until it eventually turned into the raw material the final firm needed to transform into its finished product for you, the customer.

The article of clothing you chose in question 3 above could have been made completely from a natural product − wool from sheep, cotton (a plant), or perhaps, if you are very 'dressed up' from silk. It is much more likely, though, that is will have at least some *synthetic*, or manufactured material in it, like *polyester*, *nylon* or *acrylic*. These raw materials are made originally from oil, and will have been bought by the firm which produced your clothing from an oil or chemical company, perhaps ICI, who in turn produced them from their raw material, oil, a natural product.

Survey

Compare notes with the other members of your group who answered question 3. How many people is that altogether? How many chose clothing made *only* with synthetic products? Now make two lists: one listing all the natural products used as raw materials in the clothing, and the other listing all the synthetics used. What is the most common mixture?

Find out

Why do clothing manufacturers add synthetics to their products? There are *three* reasons, and you will find a clue to one of them by comparing the washing instructions on all-natural and partly-synthetic clothes.

What goes on inside the magician's hat

So raw materials go in, and a finished product comes out. What goes on inside is a series of *processes*, gradually transforming the raw materials into the finished product.

In science lessons, you may have tried making paper from wood. First you would have chopped the wood into small pieces, then soaked it in water and boiled it until it formed a pulpy mash. Then you would have pressed this pulp, and finally dried it. Because the soaking and boiling of wood takes a long time, you might well have started with straw, but the principle is the same. You would have taken the wood through four different processes:

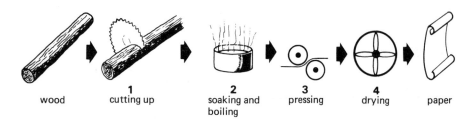

| wood | 1 cutting up | 2 soaking and boiling | 3 pressing | 4 drying | paper |

Your raw material was wood, your finished product paper. Each process requires different machinery, and each process brings the wood gradually nearer to being paper.

A *firm* manufacturing paper does much the same thing, only on a much larger scale. Also, a paper manufacturer will use various other raw materials as well as wood, like chemicals to speed up the pulp making, and bleach to make the paper white.

Notice that just as each process requires its own machinery, so it usually has its own *workers*. People generally work on one process, dealing with the raw material in the state it comes to them, and then passing it on to other workers with other machines in its new state, for the next process. This principle can be seen in its most extreme form on a *production line*, where the product being made moves on a *conveyor belt* from one process (group of workers and machines) to the next.

Fact . . . The longest indoor conveyor belt in Britain is in the British Leyland car factory at Longbridge, in Birmingham.

Anything else?

Yes. The firm needs raw materials to turn into finished products. It does this by subjecting the raw materials to a series of processes, each of which brings them closer to being the finished product — the manufactured article.

But the firm needs four other things before the process can work. Two of them we have already mentioned: the firm needs workers, and it needs machines. Workers are called *labour*, and by this we mean *everyone* who works in the firm, from the person who sweeps the floor, to the Managing Director.

Machines are part of the firm's *capital*. This is all the fixed items which the firm needs, and which stay with the firm. Capital includes the machines, the factory buildings, the land and the firm's vehicles. Raw materials are *not* capital, because they do not stay with the firm. They are processed and then sold to the firm's customers. *Capital* is sometimes called *plant*.

The third thing the firm needs is *energy* to work the machines and heat and light the factory. This energy is usually electricity, coal, oil or gas, or a combination of these. Energy, as anyone will tell you, is expensive, and many industrial processes (like those involved in making paper) use a great deal of it.

Finally, the firm needs someone, or a group of people, with the brains and the initiative to start the firm up, to expand it, to develop it, and to keep it running. This combination of brains and initiative is called *enterprise*.

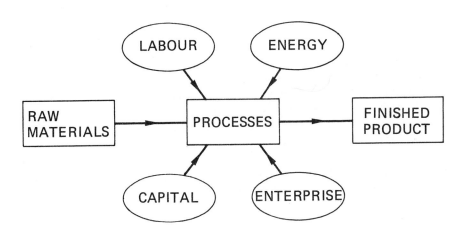

More questions

THINK

Of a firm which makes leather shoes.

1   What is the firm's *finished product*?

2   What is the firm's main *raw material*?

3   What are the main *processes* the raw material will go through before it becomes the finished product? Draw a diagram showing the processes (like we did for the manufacture of paper). Say what the raw material will have been changed to after each process.

4   What other raw materials will the firm use, apart from the one you named in question 2 above?

5   What other *four* things, apart from raw materials, will the firm need in order to manufacture its finished product? Write each one in capital letters, and then explain what it is, and why it is needed.

6   Say whether each of the following is *capital, raw material*, or *energy*:
The oil BP turns into petrol.
The oil British Leyland uses to heat its factories.
A window cleaner's chamois (shammy) leather.

7   And finally, explain the difference between a *firm*, and a *factory*.

From factory to customer

Of course, one of the essential things every firm must have is *customers*. Without customers, there would be no point in producing anything. And so one of the main questions a firm has to consider is how to get its finished products to its customers.

Another word for a customer is a *consumer*. To consume is to use, and a consumer is someone who uses a firm's products. Consumer is really a better word for us to use than customer, because the firm's customer does not always consume the goods. A large garage may buy all its cars from Ford. The garage is therefore Ford's customer, but it is not the consumer. The consumers are the people who then buy the cars from the garage to use. By *consumer* we mean the person who finally ends up using the finished product.

From factory to consumer

There are various ways the goods get from the factory to the consumer.

1   The consumer fetches them. The factory might have a shop attached to it from which consumers buy the goods. Called a 'factory shop', this is not always a good way to buy things. It can be rather fun seeing where they are made, and sometimes how they are made, but they are often rather expensive 'showrooms' for a firm's products.

2   The factory delivers them to the consumer. This is called *mail order*, because the consumer orders the goods through the post, by mail. There are several ways of doing this. The consumer could order from an advertisement, like the one shown here. Or the advertisement might have been delivered through the door (this is sometimes referred to as a 'mail shot'). Or the consumer might have seen the goods in a catalogue.

Catalogue trading

Some mail order firms send catalogues to people who answer their advertisements in newspapers. These people then become *agents* for the firm and pass their catalogues round their friends collecting orders. The orders are sent off to the firm, which pays the agents *commission* (usually 10%) on everything their customers have ordered. One big attraction of catalogues is that you can pay for your goods after receiving them at so much a week over perhaps 26 weeks, giving the money to the agent, and they charge you no more than the cash price if you do.

BUT . . . the price of goods in the catalogues is very often *higher* than you could find it in shops. And *if* you want to buy something from a catalogue, why not get the catalogue yourself directly from the firm, and thereby get the 10% commission yourself?

9

Mail order goods can often be ordered by telephone as well as by mail, or from a door-to-door salesperson, who calls at every door on the off-chance of finding a buyer. Our advice is *never* buy anything from a door-to-door salesman or woman without checking the price of whatever he or she is selling in the shops first. And if he or she is not prepared to give you a week or so to do this, you can probably guess why!

3   The factory delivers the goods to a *middleman*, who then sells them to the consumers. By far the most common way of selling goods, this method allows the factory to deliver large quantities of its products (perhaps lorryloads) to the same place, from where consumers in each local area can buy them. There are dozens of examples – Comet, Asda, Marks and Spencer, Sainsbury's – in fact virtually all our large shops. Comet is the middleman because it is in the middle, between the factory and the consumer.

   If a shop is small, it would not be worth a firm delivering a lorry load of goods to them, and they would not want to buy them in such large quantities. In such a case the firm will deliver to a local *wholesaler* who will then himself deliver to all the nearby small shops. Alternatively the shopkeepers might go to the wholesaler and collect what they want. In this case the wholesaler will be called a 'Cash and Carry'. The shopkeepers then re-sell (or retail) the goods to their own customers.

   Obviously the wholesaler will charge the retailer less than the retailer will charge the consumer. This is why goods are sometimes advertised at 'the wholesale price' to let you know they are cheaper than normal.

This process of distributing the goods from factory to consumer is called *distribution*. It is an essential feature of industrial life.

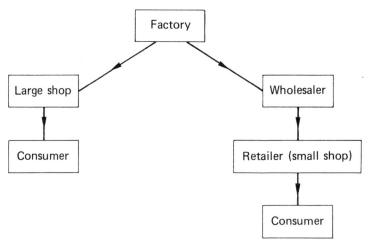

All these methods we have described are fine if a few factories are producing a lot of goods for thousands of people to buy. But suppose the goods are being produced all over the place? Can you think of any examples?

Milk, eggs, potatoes ....

Milk is a special problem to distribute. If it is not got to the consumer very quickly it goes off and becomes waste. And most consumers of milk live in cities and towns, where there are not too many cows.

These 'produced all over the place' goods usually have a special distribution service set up just to collect from the farmers and then send out to the dairies, supermarkets, greengrocers and so on. This service is called the Marketing Board. You will have heard of and seen the lorries belonging to the Milk Marketing Board.

Types of shop

Your parents will have learned as children to identify all sorts of interesting types of shops, like milliners, haberdashers, drapers, ironmongers and the like. Today shopping has changed completely. Gone are many of the small specialist shops, and in their place are much larger stores selling a wide range of goods. Much of the reason lies in a greater degree of car ownership among the population. People are now able to travel further to buy their goods, and therefore tend to go to bigger shops where prices are lower and the range of goods on sale is larger. There are still many small shops, particularly grocers selling foodstuffs, and newsagents selling newspapers, cigarettes and sweets to a local area, but the general move is to larger and larger stores. For example supermarkets, which once sold only food, now commonly sell books, clothes, plants, as well as fresh meat and fish, and it may not be long before butchers and fishmongers go the way of the milliner (who sold hats, by the way).

Large shops can themselves be sorted into 'types'.

The department store

This is a large shop, often on several floors, which is divided into different departments. Each department is almost a shop in itself, selling a particular kind of product. There might be a food department, a ladies clothes department, a gardening department, and so on.

The multiple

This shop sells only one type of product, but is part of a chain of shops across the country all with the same name, and all virtually identical. The product might be electrical goods (like Currys), clothes (like Hepworths), spares and accessories for cars and bikes (like Halfords), or furniture (like MFI). The multiple is sometimes called a *chain store*.

Inside a department store

A multiple store

A variety chain store

A hypermarket

The variety chain store

The variety chain store is like a multiple only it sells a range of goods. Woolworths is a variety chain store. Boots was a multiple when it sold mainly medicines, but has now become a variety chain store. Marks and Spencers too is getting close to being a variety chain store as it moves away from selling only clothes, and in some cases is really a department store now.

The supermarket

Originally a grocers, selling canned and packaged food, the supermarket has now expanded into all sorts of goods. The word was first used when grocers started putting their food on shelves and getting customers to help themselves, thereby saving time, space and staff. Any shop where customers collect their own purchases in a basket or trolley can properly be called a supermarket. A very large supermarket, selling a wide range of goods, with its own car park, is sometimes called a *hypermarket*. Hypermarkets are often found outside town centres.

Suggested work

1　What is *distribution*?

2　What is the difference between a customer and a consumer?

3　What are the *three* main ways in which goods go from the factory to the consumer?

4　With catalogue trading, what is the 'agent's commission'?

5　Why should you take care before buying from a catalogue or a door-to-door salesman?

6 Which of the following goods would be likely to go through a wholesaler:
   records, washing machines, socks, cars, matches? When would goods not go through a wholesaler?

7 Make a table with *four* columns headed: Department Store, Multiple, Variety Chain Store, and Supermarket. Under each heading, briefly describe that type of shop, and then list five actual shops of each type in your own town or local area.

8 Is there a hypermarket near you?

9 In what ways, and why, has the pattern of shops changed over the past fifty years? Can you see examples of this locally? And what *was* a haberdasher?

From raw material to factory

We have looked at how goods are produced, and at how they get from the factory to the consumer. But how do the raw materials get to the factory?

First, *where* do they come from? Many raw materials (like iron ore, timber, zinc, uranium) come from abroad; in particular, from Europe. In fact, more of our industry's raw materials come from Europe than from the rest of the world put together. After Europe, they come from the British Commonwealth, then the USA, then the rest of the world. So they have a long way to travel, and many of them are very heavy and bulky. If they come from abroad they will come by ship, and if they come from within Britain, they will come by train or lorry.

Where and how it gets its raw materials will affect where a firm chooses to build its factories. If by ship, it will choose a spot near a port. If by train, near a station. And if by road, near a motorway.

It may also be affected in its choice by how it distributes its finished products. If they go by post (as with some mail order companies) then it does not really matter. If they go by train or lorry, again it will have to be near a station or motorway. And since travel is expensive, it will want to be close to its consumers. The firm will have to ask itself whether it is easier to transport its raw materials or its finished products. Usually it is easier to move finished products, so it is more important to be near the source of its raw materials, but you can probably think of cases where this is not so.

Most of its consumers might actually be in one place. For example a firm supplying headlights to the motor industry will find many of its customers in the Midlands, so it would be a little silly to build a factory in Aberdeen.

15

The location of industry (where it sets up)

Some of our major cities are marked on the map, and the main motorways. The shaded areas represent coalfields.

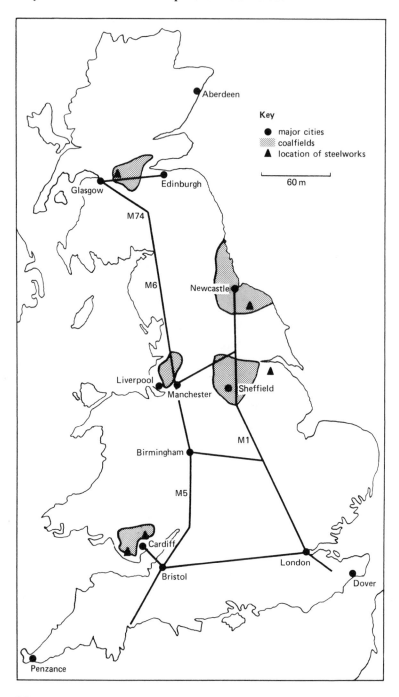

Heavy industry

So called 'heavy' industry is the factories making large goods, like ships, cars, machinery, and steel. Britain used to be the world's leader in this area of manufacture, sending finished products all over the world. It is easy to see why heavy industry set up where it did. Steel making requires coal and iron ore. Most iron ore is imported from other countries, and arrives by ship in ports such as Bristol, London, Glasgow, Liverpool and Newcastle. You can see where the coal is mined. Now where do you think the steel works would be sited? Pinpoint likely places on the map.

In fact our major steelworks are shown by the triangles on the map. Were you right? For similar reasons you can probably guess where the major ship-building yards are situated.

When it comes to making goods which, unlike ships, are meant for individual consumers, like cars, the position is somewhat different. Obviously a car factory must have steel available, but it must also take into account where its cars are going when they are built. Penzance would be an inappropriate place to build a car factory. (Look at the map.) It is nowhere near a steel works, and just as far from the major cities where most people live. London is near a lot of people, but a long way from the steelworks. Birmingham, on the other hand, is fairly well placed for both, and it is in and around Birmingham that the motor industry grew up.

For a variety of reasons, Britain no longer leads the world in the production of 'heavy' manufactured goods. Cars and ships can be built more cheaply elsewhere, and steel is made in great quantities all over Europe and throughout the world. So much so that many of our steelworks have closed or are closing. However in machines themselves, and in more complicated, 'lighter' engineering products Britain is still doing very well.

Light industry

The raw materials for 'light' industries, like electronics, plastics, and chemicals, are much easier to transport than those for the heavy industries discussed above. So it is not so important where these firms set up. However they will still take the same things into account. They will want to be near their markets, and handy for ports if they are buying or selling abroad. Because more and more of our trade is now with Europe, it is ports on the *east* coast which will be particularly handy, however.

There is therefore a change in where industry is tending to go. Areas on the west coast which were big producers of 'heavy' items are being hardest hit, and are now centres of high unemployment. Areas towards the south and east, particularly those on the motorway 'network', tend to be better off. The government is trying to encourage industry to set up in the worse-off areas though, to offset this trend.

Special development areas

Those parts of the country worst hit by the causes mentioned above have been designated 'Special Development Areas'. The government pays various grants to any firms setting up in these areas to encourage them to do so. The grants are not always enough to make a firm choose an area which it thinks is unsuitable, however, and there are examples of firms which have been persuaded and have subsequently not done very well. One such example is the car factory at Linwood, near Glasgow, which has now closed after several years of poor trading.

Suggested work

1   Copy the map of Britain, marking on it the coalfields, cities and motorways.

2   Why has the motor industry built up around Birmingham?

3   Mark on the map where you think would be good places to site the following firms:
    a warehouse of car spares brought in from France and intended for distribution around the country;
    a firm making steel lampposts for local authorities;
    a firm making bagpipes.

4   Why was there never a big steelworks near the port of London?

5   Find out where Milton Keynes is. Is this likely to be an attractive spot for light industry? Why?

6   Why did the Linwood car factory not do very well? Where do you think the firm originally wanted to put it?

7   In a further attempt to encourage industry to areas of high unemployment the government has created some 'enterprise zones'. Can you find out what these are? You could mark them together with the Development Areas on your map.

The structure of a firm

Jane to her teacher: 'How come the Principal gets paid more than you, when all he does is sit in his office all day, and you've got the job of teaching us?'

Try asking your teacher this (unless he or she *is* the Principal) and see what answer you get! Remember it is considered *very bad manners* to ask anyone *how much* they earn, unless they are a very close friend of yours.

One of the answers could be that the Principal is in charge of the whole College, and is responsible for everything that goes on in it. The Principal started as an ordinary teacher or lecturer, and has been *promoted* to a higher post because of special skills and abilities. By giving more money, the College is not only recognising responsibility, but is encouraging other teachers to get promoted, thereby trying to make sure that the best people available get the highest jobs.

But there is not just a Principal and teachers in a College or school. You probably know that some of your teachers have been promoted to other jobs, each having special responsibilities. These might include Heads of Department responsible for all the teaching in a particular subject or group of subjects; senior lecturers responsible for particular types of work; there might be an Assistant or Deputy Principal, or more than one, responsible for directly helping the Principal in his or her job.

Task

Identify the *promoted* teachers in your school or college, and say what each is responsible for. Can you arrange them in order, from the Principal down? Some will be equal — you could place them on the same line below the person or people above them.

Unless your College is very small, it could not run effectively without some of the teachers being given these special responsibilities.

The firm

The same happens in a firm. Some people are given special responsibilities, to help the firm run efficiently. In any group of workers, one will be put in charge to see that the others work properly. This person will be called a *supervisor* or *charge-hand*. If there are a number of different groups of workers, then one person will be in charge of all of them, to help the supervisors, and to deal with any problems the supervisor cannot manage. This person is often called the *foreman*. He or she is particularly important being the link between the factory 'floor', and the more senior *managers* who generally work from offices.

The foreman will report to the *Production manager*, who is in charge of all the firm's production. He or she will do far more than just see that everyone works properly though. It is also his or her job to see that the machines work as much of the time as possible, that materials are in the right places at the right times, that orders are made up when required, and to tell other managers what it is possible to produce, and when.

Other managers

There will probably be a *Sales manager* as well. He or she is responsible for selling what the firm makes, and may have responsibility for a team of sales staff. The *Personnel manager* is responsible for the recruitment and welfare of the people employed by the firm and will deal with problems about pay and conditions, and with holiday arrangements. In a firm with a large office staff, there may be an *Office manager* in charge of all the secretarial and office staff. There will probably also be a *Company secretary* or *Accountant* to deal with the financial and legal side of the business.

In a large firm

These managers will probably have assistants to help them, and there may be other managers dealing with particular aspects of a firm, like a *Customer services manager* to deal with any queries from customers. And there might be a *Research and development manager* to look at ways of improving the firm's products and methods.

The production manager in particular might have other managers working for him or her taking responsibility for different aspects of production. These could include some or all of the following.

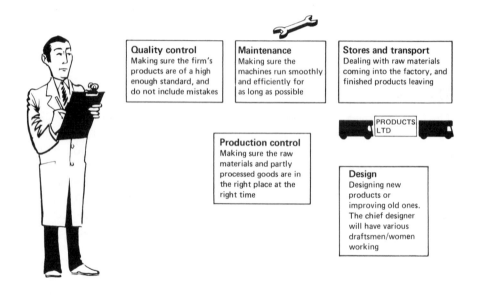

Quality control
Making sure the firm's products are of a high enough standard, and do not include mistakes

Maintenance
Making sure the machines run smoothly and efficiently for as long as possible

Stores and transport
Dealing with raw materials coming into the factory, and finished products leaving

Production control
Making sure the raw materials and partly processed goods are in the right place at the right time

Design
Designing new products or improving old ones. The chief designer will have various draftsmen/women working

The employer

There will be one person in overall charge of the firm. He or she might be called the *General manager*, or if the owner of the firm, the Proprietor. This person is like the Principal in a college, or the Headteacher in a school.

Directors

A company is owned by the shareholders. They appoint a group of people, some of whom are themselves shareholders, some of whom work for the company, to run the company on their behalf. The shareholders

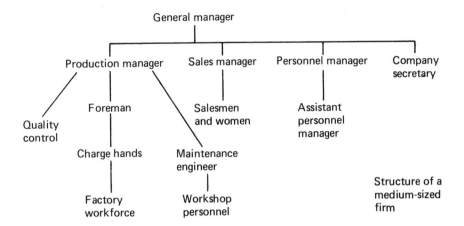

Structure of a medium-sized firm

elect these people by voting for them at the company's *Annual General Meeting* (or AGM). The people elected form the *Board of Directors* of the company. One of them will be chosen by the others to be *Chairman* of the Board. The Board of Directors meets periodically to make major decisions about the company's future, like whether and where to build new factories, what new machinery to invest in, and what new products to make.

Those directors who work for the company are called executive directors, and will each be responsible for a particular area of the company. There will be a Production director, Sales director, Personnel director, and so on.

A company might run several different firms with a number of factories, each of which will have its own structure of managers. Or it might be a small company of just one firm. In this case the managers and directors might be the same people – the Production director would also be the Production manager. However large or small the company, one of the directors will be in overall charge of the day to day running of the company; he is called the *Managing director*.

Suggested work

1   Copy out the diagram of 'the Structure of a medium-sized firm'. Make a list of the people you have included in the diagram, and by each one give a short description of their job.

2   What jobs do you think the Production manager of a large firm might have done in the past before being promoted?

3   Imagine you are the Personnel manager of a firm and have to give instructions to a new young recruit on how to treat the foreman. What would you say?

4   Which managers will have most contact, and why, with:

21

a) the factory workforce
b) the general public

5   If you were an electrical apprentice working in the maintenance section of a factory, what would your job involve? Who would probably be directly in charge of you? Who would he or she be responsible to?

Further work

Your teacher may be able to arrange for you to visit a local factory and ask them about their structure of jobs. What managers do they have? Is there a Board of Directors, and if so, where? Who is responsible for quality control? And for new recruits?

Peter Walters is the Chairman of BP

Committee meetings

We have seen that the Board of Directors and the Annual General Meeting 'decide' various things. When a group of people meet together to discuss or decide something they are usually called a *committee*. But how can a group of perhaps ten different people decide something if they do not all agree? And you know from your own experience that they probably will not all agree.

Why bother with committees?
There are three main reasons.
a) Several people might all be concerned with the matter being discussed and might all want to have their say.
b) Most decisions that are taken have to be acceptable to as many people

as possible, otherwise there will be trouble putting them into effect.

c) There is usually more chance of getting a decision right if several people 'put their heads together'.

There are two types of committee – an *advisory* committee does not actually decide anything, it only makes a *recommendation* which the person it is recommending to (perhaps the Manager concerned) does not have to accept: on the other hand an *executive* committee actually makes the decision itself. The Board of Directors is an executive committee; so is the House of Commons.

But you can imagine what might happen if a group of people all sit down and start discussing something. They might come to blows, or start talking about last night's television, or all talk at once. To stop this happening there are set rules which committees have to follow. Sometimes the committee makes its own rules – these are called *standing orders*. More usually the committee follows certain general rules, well known and accepted by everyone.

Rules of a committee

The **agenda.** This is a paper sent round before the meeting to everyone on the committee. The agenda gives the date and time and place of the meeting, and a list of the things which will be discussed, in the order they will be discussed. There is usually a place on the agenda for 'Any Other Business' to allow people to raise matters not on the agenda.

The **quorum.** There is sometimes (but not always) a minimum number of people who have to be there before the meeting can take place. In a committee of ten, the quorum might be five. So unless there are at least five people there, the meeting will be cancelled.

The **chairman.** The Chairman is the man (or woman) in charge of the meeting. He will follow the agenda exactly, and tell the people who can speak, and when. (There may be several people who all want to talk at the same time). Everyone who speaks talks to the Chairman, even if he is

"speaking through the chair"

23

really talking to someone else. A speaker might say something like: 'Mr Chairman, may I remind Mr Smith that we tried his idea last year and it did not work.' This is to stop people arguing with each other, and is called 'speaking through the chair'.

The **minutes**.   One of the people present will be the committee's *secretary*. He or she will write down the main points that are discussed, and any decisions that are reached, as a record of the meeting. This record is called the *minutes*. It is given to everyone on the committee some time after the meeting. One of the first items on the agenda of the next meeting will be the 'agreeing of the previous meeting's minutes'. This means that everyone has a chance to say if the minutes are accurate. The next item on the agenda might be 'Matters arising from the minutes'. This means that the committee can ask about anything that was in the minutes to see if things decided on actually happened.

Taking decisions

Once the committee has discussed something, a member of the committee might make a *proposal* to be decided. It could be something like: 'I propose that we build the new factory at Penzance.' Providing there is someone else who agrees, and who will *second* the proposal, the Chairman will call for a vote. If a majority of those present vote in favour, then the proposal is passed, and becomes a decision. The Chairman votes again if there is a dead heat. His vote will then decide the matter, and is called a *casting vote*.

The veto

Very occasionally, someone on the committee has the power to *veto* any proposal. This means that however many people vote in favour of a proposal, even if everyone except him does, his one vote against will cause the proposal to be defeated. Vetoes are rather rare. Britain has the power of veto in the United Nations Security Council, and used it in the vote over a proposal during the Falklands crisis.

Here is a sample agenda for a meeting of a firm's social committee:

Meeting of Social Committee next Tuesday 23rd at 2.30pm in Mr Black's office

Agenda

1. Apologies for Absence
2. Minutes of last meeting to be agreed
3. Matters arising from minutes
4. Proposed Christmas dance
5. Report of outing to Westlake Distillery
6. Financial report from Treasurer
7. A.O.B. (Any Other Business)

Suggested work

1   You should know what the various words we have used mean:
    Advisory and executive committees
    Agenda
    Quorum
    Chairman
    Speaking through the Chair
    Minutes
    Proposal (this is sometimes also called a *motion*)
    Seconding a proposal
    Chairman's casting vote
    Veto

2   However it is more important that you gain some practice in how committees work by actually trying it out. Try working in groups of six or seven. Choose a Chairman and Secretary. Take as your agenda a topic of interest to all of you: something to propose about the workings of your College or school, for example – dinner arrangements, changes in the course, a social outing . . . . . You will be an advisory committee of course.
Talk about your topic according to the rules, make a proposal (properly seconded) and produce the minutes.
You'll soon get the hang of it.

3   Listen to a real committee in action. The House of Commons is a sort of committee and you can listen to some of their debates. Notice that they all talk to the Speaker (that's what they call the Chairman), who tells each person when they can talk.

Sample multiple choice questions

1   Capital investment in a business means spending money on:
    a) raw materials
    b) advertising
    c) replacing machinery
    d) Directors' fees

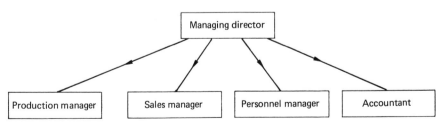

2   In the above diagram, to which Manager would a maintenance technician be responsible?

25

a) Production manager
b) Sales manager
c) Personnel manager
d) Accountant

3 The shareholders in a public company
a) work in the company
b) manage the company
c) own the company
d) buy the goods the company produces

4 The Chairman's casting vote is used
a) when he or she wants to send someone out of a meeting
b) when the committee's vote is a dead heat
c) when he or she wants to make the committee do what he wants
d) when he or she wishes to resign

5 The machinery, vehicles and plant in a factory make up the
a) raw materials
b) processes
c) enterprise
d) capital

6 Most of Britain's raw materials are imported from
a) Europe
b) USA
c) Africa
d) Asia

7 The main responsibility of the Personnel department is to
a) supervise the workforce
b) make up the wages
c) recruit and train staff
d) advertise the firm's products

8 In a committee meeting, the secretary's main function is to
a) write the minutes
b) write the agenda
c) make the casting vote
d) second the proposals

9 Which of the following chains of distribution is *not* correct?
a) Producer − wholesaler − retailer − consumer
b) Wholesaler − producer − retailer − consumer
c) Producer − retailer − consumer
d) Wholesaler − retailer − consumer

10 Which one of the following is a distribution network?
a) a marketing board
b) a trade union

c) a consumer's association
d) an employer's organisation

11 A shop selling mainly one type of product, with branches all over the country is called a
a) hypermarket
b) variety chain store
c) multiple
d) department store

12 A raw material could be described as
a) a pure substance
b) the starting point for a manufacturing process
c) a finished product
d) a by-product

13 Which of the following has encouraged the growth of the hypermarket?
a) increased car ownership
b) high turnover
c) high rise buildings
d) increased petrol prices

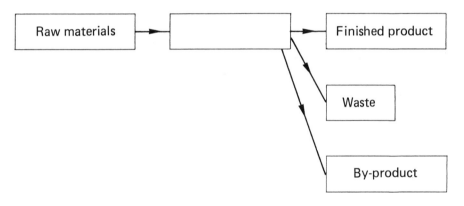

14 In the above diagram, what would go in the empty box?
a) capital
b) enterprise
c) processes
d) labour

15 Mail order refers to
a) distribution through the post
b) a marketing board
c) payment through the recorded delivery service
d) the agent's commission

3
Protection

Safety at work

When you go to work you will be in an unfamiliar and possibly dangerous situation. The firm which you work for will be partly responsible for looking after your safety, but you will also be expected to look after yourself. Your safety is a *joint* responsibility, shared between you, your employer, and the other people who work there with you.

This joint responsibility was spelt out in the *Health and Safety at Work Act*, which became law in 1974. The law says that every employee has a legal duty to take all steps to safeguard his or her own health and safety, and the health and safety of those around. The law also says that the employer too must take all steps to protect those working in the firm. This means that proper safety equipment must be provided, machines must be guarded, and any special compulsory safety measure (like those involved in welding) must be adhered to. In addition, every firm with more than twenty employees must appoint one of the employees as the 'Safety Officer' to take particular responsibility for all aspects of safety.

There is a special board – the Health and Safety Executive – to oversee the workings of the Act, and the factory inspectors visit firms to make sure they are complying with the regulations.

Note that it is the firm's responsibility to provide safety equipment, but it is the worker's responsibility to see that it is used. That is what we mean by a *joint* responsibility.

All play their part

This chain was broken over *three hundred times a day* in 1981, resulting in over 100 deaths in manufacturing industry alone.

Suggested work

What types of industry would you expect to be the most dangerous?

Divide a page in your workbook into *four* columns. In the first column list these four types of industry: Construction, Retailing (selling), Chemical manufacture, and Electrical engineering. In the second column, describe briefly what work each type of industry is engaged in. In the third column, give the names of any of your local firms engaged in this work. In the final column say how you think accidents might be caused in the type of work involved.

We will now look at some of the more common causes of accidents at work.

1. Lifting

Types of injury: damage to back
damage to hands
damage to toes and feet

Damage to back
200 people every day manage to 'slip a disc' usually by lifting something too heavy for them, or by lifting something wrongly. Think of your backbone, or spine, as a column of cotton reels, joined by a piece of elastic down the centre. If the column is *straight*, it will withstand great pressure. But if it is *curved*, the cotton reels can easily slip out of place. This is what happens when someone 'slips a disc'. A slipped disc is very painful, and sometimes never really heals properly.

Pressure

Pressure

Disc can slip out of place

No damage

WRONG ✗

RIGHT ✓

So the *golden rule* when lifting is: *Keep your back straight*. Use your leg muscles to provide the power for your lifting.

Damage to hands and feet
Strangely enough many injuries from lifting happen because the person is lifting something too heavy or too awkward for them, and therefore drops it on their toe! This can also happen because the thing being lifted has a sharp edge which cuts into the person's hand, again causing them to drop it. This is very easily done.

The *golden rule* is: Use protective boots or shoes when lifting heavy objects and if an object has sharp edges, wear gloves to protect your hands.

2. Machinery

Machinery is made up of moving parts. This simple fact accounts for many injuries caused by machines, where people get their hair, clothes, fingers or legs trapped between moving parts. You can probably think of many examples:

Long hair trapped round a drill
Fingers trapped in a grindstone
Feet caught in a conveyor belt
Clothing pulled into gear wheels or rollers

The *golden rule* is: Keep well away from moving parts, and when near to machines, keep long hair tied back, and keep loose clothing under control (for example by wearing overalls).

Remember that machines are far stronger than you are; that is why they are built — to do jobs that human muscles alone are not powerful enough to do.

You can also be injured by the machine doing to *you* what it is supposed to do to a piece of metal. This is a particular hazard with saws and guillotines. Unfortunately a guillotine cannot tell the difference between your finger and a piece of steel. Most machines are *guarded* to prevent this from happening; by having only a small gap to push the piece of work through, for example, or by having a cover to stop you falling on to a saw blade. These guards only work, of course, when they are in place, and are useless if the operator moves the guard to help him see better, or to help him move the work around more easily, or to repair the machine.

The *golden rule* is: Never operate a machine with the guard removed, and always take great care in any case to keep your fingers and hands away from cutting edges.

Finally, injury can be caused by the *debris*, or bits of waste, coming flying off high speed machines − a shower of red hot sparks from an electric saw, for instance. An operator of such a machine should always be issued with safety glasses or a visor.

The *golden rule* is: Always wear the eye protectors provided. (Revision question: 'Whose responsibility is it to *provide* the eye protectors?')

3. Dangerous conditions

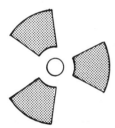

The radiation symbol

There is a reprocessing factory on the West Cumbrian coast at Windscale, Sellafield Works, run by British Nuclear Fuels. This factory takes in the used-up fuel from nuclear power stations and reprocesses it into fresh uranium, plutonium and radioactive waste products. Potentially it is a highly dangerous business dealing with extremely poisonous and very radioactive materials and the workers at Sellafield have very strict safety rules. Each time they enter the reprocessing area they are given special clothes and each time they leave, their clothing is specially monitored to ensure they have not picked up any radioactivity.

Sellafield is an extreme example, but very many factories all over the country work with dangerous materials of one sort of another.

Breathing in *asbestos* dust can injure your lungs and anyone working with asbestos at home or at work should wear a *breathing mask* which is like a pad of cotton wool strapped over your nose and mouth to filter the air.

Asbestos dust is particularly dangerous, but it is unhealthy to work in *any* dusty atmosphere for long periods. Damping down the material with water cuts down the dust, as does having plenty of fresh air.

Working with *chemicals* or *paints* can also be dangerous, both from the point of view of explosions (don't smoke if you are told not to!), and from breathing in the fumes. Face masks are sometimes worn, and rubber gloves to protect the skin from contact with chemicals. Fresh air is again very important.

An asbestos mark

British Nuclear Fuels factory, Sellafield

A *noisy* factory may seem more unpleasant than dangerous, but constant loud noise can cause permanent damage to hearing. Your body has a built-in early warning system: when the noise stops, if your ears are 'ringing', then the noise level is too high for you. (This applies to 'discos' as well as factories!) Workers in noisy surroundings are issued with *ear protectors*. It is essential to wear such protectors; even soldiers now wear them on firing ranges to defend their ears from the noise of their guns' firing.

Ear protectors

Golden rules: Always wear protective masks, ear protectors, and gloves, when these are issued. If you are working in dusty conditions, or with paint or chemicals, make sure your working area is well ventilated.

Suggested work

1 Go back through the above section and collect together the 'golden rules'. Write these down to give you a set of 'Safety Rules' for safe working.

2 Suggest *four* reasons why an operator might remove the guard on a machine.

3 Fred Smith hurts his eyes by carrying out a welding operation without wearing the face mask his employers gave him. Is this injury Fred's fault or his employers? Would it make a difference to your answer if Fred had not been issued with a face mask?

   Susan Wilkes, an experienced welder, was watching Fred, but did nothing to warn him of the dangers of not wearing his face mask. Is Susan guilty of anything under the Health and Safety at Work Act?

4 You might like to design a poster or handout warning employees of the dangers of lifting things incorrectly, or of working in dusty conditions.

Safety at home

It is not only at work that accidents happen, of course. Many people are killed or injured in their own homes. Roughly fifteen people every week die in fires, and twelve by drowning. Ten children each week die as the result of other accidents in and around the home, and this is therefore the greatest single cause of childhood deaths. Below we outline some of the main causes of these accidents and how to avoid or deal with them. As you work your way through this section you will learn the general principles of *First Aid*.

First Aid means what it says. It is the *first* bit of help you give if you are at the scene of an accident. It is the help you give while you are waiting for a doctor or ambulance to arrive. The purpose of First Aid is to keep an accident victim alive until medical help arrives. You cannot substitute for a doctor, but you can make sure the doctor still has a patient to treat when he or she arrives.

The main causes of death from accidents in the home are *Suffocation* and *Choking, Bleeding, Fire,* and *Electrocution.* We will now look at how to avoid each of these, and at what to do if an accident should occur.

A breath of air

We need air to keep us alive, and lack of air even for a few minutes, is likely to be fatal. We can lose our air supply either because our windpipe, or mouth and nose become blocked, or because our lungs stop working. Blocking our windpipe is called *choking,* and blocking our mouth and nose is *suffocation.*

Common causes of *choking*: Food, or small objects stuck in the windpipe. Babies are particularly at risk from picking up and trying to swallow small toys, boiled sweets, marbles, etc.

Action: 1 Slap victim on back
If that doesn't work
          2 If a small child, hold upside down and slap child hard on the back. If a larger person, bend them over and slap them hard on the back
If that doesn't work
          3 Try to remove object from throat with your finger
If that doesn't work
          4 Punch victim in stomach
If that doesn't work
          5 Call an ambulance immediately, and keep trying 2, 3 and 4.

Common causes of *suffocation*: For a child: Putting head in a polythene bag, or if a baby, sleeping head down on a soft pillow, or sleeping with a dog or cat

For an adult: Very rare; really caused only by smoke or gas or by drowning.

Action: Remove cause of suffocation, or remove victim from smoke or gas. You will usually be too late though, so make sure these accidents do not happen in the first place. In the case of a victim of smoke or gas suffocation, call a doctor.

Lungs stopped working? See section on 'After an Accident' later on.

A drop of blood

There are two types of bleeding – *surface* bleeding and *arterial* bleeding. Surface bleeding is not serious and can be stopped with a plaster or bandage, preferably with some *antiseptic cream* on it, to keep the cut free from germs. The cut should be cleaned in water, using cotton wool to dab the skin if dirty and then dried with cotton wool before fixing the plaster. If the cut is deep, the victim should be taken to the doctor to see if any stitches are needed to hold the skin together, or if an anti-tetanus injection is needed.

Arterial bleeding, though, is very serious indeed. This is where blood is pumped from the heart out of a deep cut because the cut has punctured an *artery*. You can tell arterial bleeding because the blood is dark coloured and comes out in spurts. Arterial bleeding must be stopped *immediately*.

Action: 1 Remove any obvious large object, like a piece of glass, from the wound.
2 Press hard on the wound to stop the bleeding. Use a handkerchief or pad of material to help and if the bleeding does not stop, move the pad around slightly, or press harder, until it does.
3 Call an ambulance.

Fire and smoke

Fire and smoke are real killers. Smoke can kill by suffocation, and fire by burning. Fires in the home are usually caused by one of the following:

Carelessness with matches and cigarettes (300 deaths and injuries are caused each year by people smoking in bed)
Electrical faults
Fire spreading from open coal or electric fires
Fat in a chip pan catching fire from overheating
In addition, burns and scalds are frequently caused by:
Giving babies drinks too hot for them
Children pulling saucepans or kettles off the cooker or worksurface
Spilling boiling water
Touching hot surfaces, such as cookers or irons

Action: General: Be prepared for a possible house fire. Make sure everyone in the house knows how to get out, and that they will not be trapped by doors they cannot open or unlock. Do you have a fire extinguisher at home? Or a smoke detector?
If there is a fire, get everyone out first, *then* call the fire brigade.
If clothing catches fire: wrap the victim in a blanket, rug or curtain. Don't put a mirror above an open fire (Why not?)
If a chip pan catches fire: do not try to move it, and *never* throw water on it (it will explode). Turn off the heat, and cover the pan with a damp cloth, or a lid. This will put out the flames.

Treatment for burns and scalds
A *scald* is a burn caused by boiling or hot liquids, like water.
Immediately place burn or scald under cold running water
Cover burn with a clean, dry cloth or dressing
Do not try to remove clothing from burnt skin, unless the clothing is soaked with petrol
If the burn is large, or serious, take the victim to the doctor.

Hazard spotting

Can you spot the possible dangers of fire, burns or scalds in this kitchen?

Gas

There are some special safety rules relating to *gas*; gas can kill by explosion, fire or suffocation.

Always   if you smell gas and suspect a leak, turn off the gas at the mains, open the windows, and call the gas board (under 'Gas' in the 'phone book). It goes without saying that you should never hunt for a gas leak with a match!

Always   if the gas supply goes off for any reason, perhaps because you have a coin meter, or have turned off the mains switch, turn off *all* your gas taps and appliances before you insert more money, or turn the mains supply back on again.

Never   leave a gas fire on when you are out of the house or go to bed at night. Boilers and water heaters which are designed to be left on permanently have special safety devices to turn themselves off if the gas supply is interrupted, or if the flames go out.

A bit of a shock

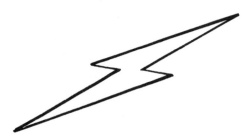

There are two different types of shock, *electric shock* and *accident shock*.

Electric shock

The human body does not like electricity. A tiny current passing through your body will give you a nasty shock, and may kill you. You do not need to be struck by lightning to be electrocuted — there is quite enough power in an ordinary socket.

When this electric appliance is turned on, current flows from the *live* terminal in the plug along the brown wire and into the appliance. After working the light, radio, or whatever, the current then flows back to the *neutral* terminal in the plug along the blue wire.

All the time the current is looking for an easy way out — a way of returning to earth. If you touch a live wire or terminal, the current will seize the opportunity to return to earth through you, giving you a shock, or worse, on the way. Notice that if the wall socket is turned on, then whether the appliance is turned on or not, both the brown (live) wire and anything in the appliance before its switch will be live with electricity. The plastic coating over the wires, and the covers over the metal terminals in the appliance, are to *insulate* the metal bits and stop you from touching them. If the insulation in an appliance breaks down, then all the metal in it can become live. This is why many appliances have an *earth* wire (green and yellow striped) so that the current will return to earth along this wire instead of through you.

Can you therefore see why:

1 If you connect a switch into the lead going to an appliance, the wire the switch actually operates (if it is not both of them) *must* be the brown wire.
2 If you are tampering with the insides of anything electrical, you *must* turn the appliance off at the wall socket, not just at the switch on the appliance. (It is better still to take the plug out completely, just to be sure.)
3 It is very dangerous to do anything at all to anything electrical unless you know exactly what you are doing.

Wiring a plug
Since the live, neutral and earth wires do very different things, it is obviously essential to connect them up to the right terminals in the plug. Quite apart from being dangerous, connecting the wires wrongly will damage most electrical equipment. (But not all, some appliances will work normally with the wires the wrong way round, but will still be potentially dangerous – the fact that it is working does not make it safe.) Looking at a plug from the top: live – brown, neutral – blue and earth – green and yellow.

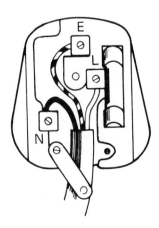

On some older appliances you may find the old colour coding: live – red, neutral – black, earth – green.

Fuses

Fuses give *absolutely no protection whatsoever* against electric shock. It would take far more current to blow even a 3 amp fuse than it would take to kill you. The fuse is there to protect the appliance and the wires from damage and fire caused by a sudden high current. It is important to use the right fuse because if the fuse value is too low, the fuse will blow before the appliance will work. On the other hand, if the fuse value is too high, then a current may melt the wires or damage the appliance before the fuse blows. Things that will work off low currents have thin, light wires, and require 3 amp fuses. Things which need a higher current to work them have thick wires and 13 amp fuses.

How do I know which fuse to use? In general, things which do not heat up need 3 amp fuses to protect their thin wires. Lights, amplifiers, radios, clocks and small, or black and white televisions are such appliances. Electric kettles, toasters, fires and such like, however, need a higher current to work them and therefore have thicker wires and 13 amp fuses. If in doubt, look at the appliance itself. It is almost certain to give somewhere a *rating*, either in *amps* (less than 3 amps and it should have a 3 amp fuse), or in *watts*. Anything less than 500 watts (500W) should have a 3 amp fuse.

Action: 1 Make sure you wire appliances up correctly, using the right fuse.
2 Never touch the insides of an appliance, or any terminals, without taking the plug out of the wall socket.
3 If any insulation is wearing off electric wires, or is damaged, replace the wire. Do not use insulating *tape* to join power leads together — it comes off too easily. Either use a complete new piece of wire, or buy proper connectors.

If an accident does happen: 1 Switch off current. If this is impossible, move the victim away from the supply — but don't touch the victim, use something wooden, or some dry cloths.
2 The victim may have burns (see above section), or may have stopped breathing (see below).

After an accident

Stop serious (arterial) bleeding, check breathing, treat for accident shock.

Victim stopped breathing

It is not always easy to tell if someone is breathing. It is easy to tell if a person definitely *is* breathing, but extremely difficult to be sure that they aren't. One way is to hold a mirror to their mouth; it will cloud over if they are breathing. If you have not got a mirror on you, you can tell by putting your cheek next to their mouth; you should feel their breath. If you are not sure, assume they have stopped breathing.

Someone who has stopped breathing will die quickly. They may well still be alive, though, and you should always remember that you cannot tell whether they are alive, but not breathing, or dead, so you hope for the best, and try and get their breathing started again. This is done by mouth-to-mouth resuscitation. A book is no substitute for a practical demonstration of this, but the basic idea is that you blow the air you are breathing out (which still has plenty of oxygen left in it) into the victim's lungs. Their lungs will breathe out automatically, making themselves ready to receive your next 'blow'.

The only problem with this is to make sure that the air actually gets to the victim's lungs. Two things could stop it: there might be some obstruction in the mouth (clear it out with your fingers); and the victim's tongue could have fallen back and blocked the windpipe. To clear the tongue out of the way, lift the victim's neck and gently bend his head back. Then hold his nose (otherwise the air will escape through it), and blow away!

You really need to practise putting someone in this position, and practise blowing into a dummy's mouth (you have to blow quite hard).

Accident shock

After any accident, the victim may be in a state of shock. This type of shock should not be confused with *electric* shock, although a victim of electric shock may also suffer from accident shock. Shock is a state of collapse − the body is no longer working properly. Shock is very dangerous if left untreated. The victim will be cold, clammy and frightened.

Action: 1 Keep the victim warm, covering him or her with coats or blankets. If the person's injuries are not serious, give them something hot to drink, like a cup of tea (but *never* alcohol, which makes shock worse). If the injuries are serious, the person may need an operation, which will be delayed if you have given them food or drink.

2 Reassure the victim. Tell him or her that he or she will be all right.

3 *Never* leave the victim alone. Wherever you are in Britain it is virtually certain that help will arrive of its own accord sooner or later.

Remember, if an accident does happen . . . . . bleeding, breathing, shock.

Suggested work

1 What is the meaning of 'First Aid'?

2 If a pan of fat catches fire, what action should you take?

3 What is the correct treatment for a burn or scald?

4 What advice would you give to the mother of a young child to help prevent her child being suffocated?

5 Copy out this diagram of a plug, and write in the colour of the wire going to each terminal. You must know these by heart. Try testing a friend.

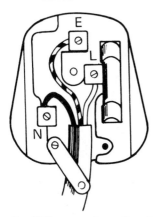

6 Why are plugs fitted with fuses? When would you use a 13 amp rather than a 3 amp fuse?

7 Write out a list of instructions telling someone how to give mouth-to-mouth resuscitation.

8 What is accident shock? How is it treated?

9 Look at these *three* situations. Say what you would do in each case, and how the accident could have been avoided in the first place.

Situation 1

Situation 1 After playing with a small toy, a young child is seen gasping for breath.

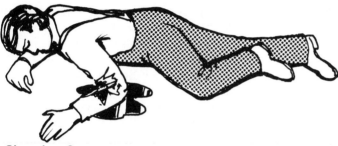

Situation 2

Situation 2 After an accident with a factory guillotine, a workman falls unconscious to the floor with blood spurting out from a gash in his arm.

Situation 3

Situation 3 A young woman is standing in front of the fire doing her make-up, when her dress catches fire and goes up in flames.

*A fuller treatment of many of the issues raised so far in this chapter, together with coverage of safety on the roads, may be found in the book 'Safety at Home, at Work and In between', published by Edward Arnold 1978.

Insurance

It is obviously best to prevent fires and accidents from happening and with care and forethought this can often be done. However, accidents do happen and we must be prepared for them in order to suffer as little as possible. That is why you should be familiar with *First Aid*, to help keep injuries as slight as possible. It is also the reason for *Insurance*, which is designed to keep financial losses from accidents as small as possible.

Principle of insurance

The principle behind insurance is that you pay a small amount to an insurance company each year (called the *premium*) to cover yourself against some particular accident, or *risk*. If the risk you are insured against happens, then the insurance company will pay your losses for you. For example millions of people insure their houses against the risk they will burn down. From the money taken in these millions of small premiums, an insurance company can afford to pay the full cost of rebuilding the few houses which do burn down. Because there is only a small risk of your house burning down, the premium will be relatively small.

However the more it would cost to rebuild your house, the higher your premium will be. Premiums are worked out at so much per £1000 of cover. (*Cover* is the amount the insurance company will pay out.) The typical premium for insuring a house against fire is £1.50 per £1000: in other words, if your house would cost £23 000 to rebuild, the premium would be £1.50 × 23, or £34.50 each year.

When house insurance first started, the insurance companies gave their clients a metal badge to attach to their house to show it was insured. In those days the only fire service was run by the insurance companies, and they would only put out fires in houses showing their own badge! You can still very occasionally see these 'fire marks' on old houses.

You can insure against almost any risk at all, remembering that the more likely it is to happen, the more the premium will be. Film stars have insured their bodies against damage, footballers their legs, and vicars have insured their church fêtes against the risk of rain. A pregnant woman can even insure herself against having twins! In general, you can only insure yourself against a risk that will cost you money if it happens (a pregnant woman would have to buy a new double pram if she had twins), and you can only insure yourself for what you will actually lose. You cannot make a profit out of insurance, you can only cover a loss.

Common types of insurance you might consider

House buildings   Covers the buildings of your house against fire and various other risks. If you live in a rented house, the person you are renting it from will be responsible for this.

> ESSENTIAL IF YOU OWN YOUR
> HOUSE – UNNECESSARY
> OTHERWISE

House contents   Covers all the furniture and belongings in your house against fire, theft, accidental damage (you drop the TV set) and getting lost. Most Contents Insurance also covers *Personal Liability* as well. This means any damage you cause to someone else's property, by, for example, stepping off the pavement and thereby making a car drive into a lamppost to avoid you.

Typical premium: £4.50 per £1000 of cover. The contents of your home are probably worth far more than you think; most people have between £5000 and £10 000 worth of cover. How much would £5000 worth of cover cost at £4.50 per £1000?

45

Note: It is possible to get House Contents Insurance without accidental damage cover for a lower premium. Unless you have nothing of value which could get easily broken (most unlikely — even a carpet can get accidentally damaged) this is probably not a good idea.

> ESSENTIAL

All risks Covers personal possessions against loss, theft or damage. This is only really applicable if you do not live at home, and therefore do not have any house contents to insure. It would cover clothes, jewellery, a radio, books, bicycle, etc.
Typical premium: £5.50 per £100 of cover, but varies considerably.

> A GOOD IDEA IF YOU LIVE
> AWAY FROM HOME —
> UNNECESSARY OTHERWISE

Vehicle insurance Covers a car or motorbike, and the driver against various risks depending on the particular policy. The minimum vehicle insurance covers you against injuries you might cause to other road users.

46

This type of insurance is compulsory and is called Road Traffic Act insurance, but is rare because it would leave you to pay any damage you caused to someone else's car (which might cost a considerable amount) yourself. A much better bet is *Third Party* insurance which also covers you for damage you cause to other people's property. Better still is *Third Party Fire and Theft* which covers you against your car being stolen or catching fire too, and costs very little more than Third Party on its own.

You can also cover yourself against damage you do to your own car, by taking out a *Comprehensive* policy. This is *much* more expensive than Third Party Fire and Theft, and is only worth it if your vehicle is relatively new, and therefore valuable.

ESSENTIAL AND
COMPULSORY BY LAW

No claims bonus With car insurance, and sometimes motorbike insurance, the insurance company will give you a discount if you did not claim from them during the previous year. After one year's claim-free driving the discount is around 20%, after two years 40%, after three years 50%, and after four years (the maximum) 60%. You can also get a discount if you say that only you will drive the car (plus your husband or wife), or if you offer to pay the first £25 or £50 of any claim yourself (called an 'excess').

47

Typical premiums: Premiums are higher for young drivers, for fast or expensive cars, and for certain parts of the country (like the big cities). They also vary a lot from company to company. For an 18 year old driving a Ford Cortina in say, Yorkshire, the premium might be £650 a year for Comprehensive cover or £250 a year for Third Party Fire and Theft. For a 22 year old with four years' No Claims Discount the £650 would immediately be reduced by 60% to £260, and the £250 to £100. It is well worth driving carefully!

Life assurance   There are three different types of life assurance.

1 *Term policy*   This assurance pays out a sum of money if you die within a set time, which could be 10, 20 or 30 years. The idea is to protect a family if the breadwinner dies, particularly if they have a mortgage to pay. If you do not die within the term you get nothing. The premiums depend on age, but are quite small, perhaps £2 a month for £20 000 insurance over 20 years.

> ESSENTIAL IF YOU HAVE
> A FAMILY TO PROTECT –
> UNNECESSARY OTHERWISE

2 *Endowment insurance with profits policy*   This assurance pays out if you die, like term insurance, but it also pays out if you are still alive at the end of the term. The amount it pays if you are still alive is less than what it pays if you die, but the sum is boosted by the company's profits each year. Since the company is bound to pay out one way or another, the premiums are much higher than with term insurance. Endowment insurance is really very long term saving, and you should only take it out if you really want to save for something 20 or 30 years in the future, and if you are sure you will still be able to afford the premiums in the years to come. Typical premium? Perhaps £15 a month for £10 000 insurance over 20 years.

> ONLY WORTHWHILE IF
> YOU WANT VERY LONG
> TERM SAVINGS – THINK
> CAREFULLY

3 *Endowment insurance without profits policy* This assurance is like the previous type, but the sum is not boosted by the firm's profits. Slightly cheaper, but not nearly as good as a savings scheme, and again, nowhere near as good as term insurance for protection. Often sold by salespeople to young people – watch out!

> STEER WELL
> CLEAR

How to insure

If you want to take out insurance, you can either go to an Insurance Broker, or direct to one or more Insurance Companies. The broker has details of all the major companies and will try and find the best one for you. Of course he or she is paid by the Insurance Companies for selling their policies and may take this into account when he or she advises you. It is best, if you want to deal with the companies yourself, to get quotes from two or three different ones. When you have decided on your company, you will fill in a *Proposal form* giving various details about yourself relevant to the insurance concerned. If the company is satisfied they will accept you, and issue you with the *policy*. This states exactly all the terms of your insurance and should be read very carefully to make sure it meets your needs. If it does, you can complete the insurance by paying the first premium. You are then covered against the risk.

Suggested work

1 Explain the following terms: premium, risk, cover, policy.

2 Fred Smith is 18 and has just passed his driving test. He has bought a twelve year old Mini and wishes to insure it. What insurance would you advise him to take out?

3 The Begun's house would cost £28 000 to rebuild. How much would it cost them to insure against fire at typical rates?

4 Annemarie Melman is a 17 year old student living in 'digs' away from home. She is single, and has no insurances of any kind. One day a salesman calls and offers her an endowment type of Life Insurance (without profits) at a very cheap price. Should she take him up on it? Can you suggest any other insurance she might think about getting? How should she go about it?

5   Mr Awale is a married man with two young children. He has a house he is buying with a mortgage of £15 000. He estimates his house would cost £32 000 to rebuild if it were burnt down. He has a three year-old Vauxhall Cavalier. What insurance policies would you recommend him to take out, and why?

Sample multiple choice questions

1   Under the Health and Safety at Work Act 1974 an employer with more than 20 employees must
    a) appoint a safety officer
    b) contribute to the Health and Safety Executive
    c) offer Health Insurance to his employees
    d) employ a company doctor

2   Which of the following is suitable protective clothing for use with asbestos?
    a) safety glasses
    b) steel toe caps
    c) overalls
    d) a breathing mask

3   The main reason why very young children should not be given small toys is
    a) they can get easily lost
    b) they are likely to be swallowed
    c) the child will be unable to manipulate them
    d) they can be thrown

4   If a chip pan catches fire, what is the correct course of action?
    a) cover the pan with a damp cloth
    b) cover the pan with a cloth and take it outside
    c) turn off the heat and cover the pan with a cloth
    d) pour water on the flames

5   The job of a factory inspector is to
    a) ensure minimum wages are paid
    b) ensure training facilities are adequate
    c) ensure safety regulations are met
    d) ensure quality control

6   Which of the following colours identifies the *live* wire?
    a) brown
    b) blue
    c) black
    d) green and yellow striped

7   What type of fire would it not be suitable to use a water extinguisher on?

a) paper
b) wood
c) clothing
d) petrol

8 Which of the following organizations is responsible for the operation of the Health and Safety at Work Act?
a) The Health Education Council
b) The Regional Health Boards
c) The Health and Safety Executive
d) The Health Centre

9 If an accident victim is found to be bleeding badly, the first action
taken should be to
a) dial 999
b) attempt to stop the bleeding
c) give artificial respiration.
d) treat for shock.

10 The details of an insurance contract are given in the
a) premium
b) endowment
c) policy
d) discount

11 When looking at an open plug while wiring it up, the terminal on the
left is the
a) live
b) neutral
c) positive
d) earth

12 A small burn or scald should be treated by
a) bathing in salt water
b) bandaging with cream
c) smoothing on cream
d) placing under a running tap

13 Which of the following assurance policies would be most suitable
for a man wanting to protect his family in the event of his death?
a) term
b) endowment with profits
c) endowment without profits
d) health

14 The most likely injury caused by lifting incorrectly is to the
a) arm
b) hand
c) elbow
d) back

15 The responsibility for safety at work is borne by
  a) the employer
  b) the employee
  c) both of these
  d) both of these together with all other employees

4

More about firms

How factories began — the Industrial Revolution

7 Highclose Cottages,
Shepsey.
12th June, 1782

Dear Mary,

Thankyou for your letter. We are all well here, but are not doing as well
as we were with the cloth making. As you know Tom has a loom in the
upstairs room to weave the cloth, and our two eldest and myself spin
the cotton on our 'spinning jenny' downstairs. 'Jenny' is a short word
we use for 'engine'. Thank goodness young David is now four, and able
to earn his keep helping young Susan brush the cotton ready for spinning.
But Mr Tomkins, who brings us the cotton each Saturday and collects
our finished cloth at the same time, has dropped the amount he pays us
yet again. He says he has trouble selling the finished cloth in Manchester
because the new factories are making it so much more more cheaply on
their fancy new machines. You asked him if we could'nt have one of
Arkwright's spinning frames here to replace the old 'jenny' but he
just laughed and said even if we could afford it it would'nt fit into
the house, and what's more it needs a horse or a water wheel to
power it! I don't know how we're going to manage if this goes on.
I suppose you're quite grateful for the cheap cloth because I remember

you complaining about the price of clothes at last year's fair, but it means we have to work on Mondays too, which we never used to, only taking Sundays off if we are to produce enough cloth even to live on.

Tom was saying the other day that he might stop weaving if Fred, who is now nearly fourteen, can manage the loom on his own, and get a job on the new canal they're building near us. He would be called a 'navigator', or 'navvy', and would get paid for his labour — not a lot but an improvement on what we get now.

Well I must close now. It's getting too dark to see and I don't want to light a candle since I think Tom has almost finished and then we'll all be going to bed.

Love to Bill and the children, Ever yours,

Janet

What was Janet talking about?

First, her letter is completely made up. Everything in it could have been true for a weaver's family in 1782, but she would not have written it. It is most unlikely Janet would have been able to read, and even less likely that she would have been able to write. Neither she nor her children would have gone to school. Even if she had been able to read and write she would probably not have written a letter because her friend Mary would not have been able to pay the postage. In those days the person getting the letter paid for it, and it was not cheap.

Leaving that aside, let us look at what she said. She and her family were *domestic* workers, which means they worked together *at home*. At that time most people did, whether they were weaving cotton or wool, making stockings (common in Leicestershire, Nottinghamshire and Derbyshire), or nails (as in the Midlands). Merchants would take the raw cotton, wool, rods of iron or whatever to people's homes, and collect the finished work. All the family would help. This is an example of *specialization*, with each family doing one job. Not only does each family have special skills though, they also have special *machines* to help them with their work. These machines had developed gradually over hundreds of years and were often provided by the merchants.

A machine is simply a collection of wheels, axles, levers and pulleys put together to help someone do a particular job. The first machines were concerned with producing food — ploughs, millstones to grind corn, pumps to move water for example. Later machines were invented and built by people in all manner of occupations. Machines continued the gradual progress that specialization had started — the creation of more wealth and more surplus by increasing the work that one person could do.

At the time Janet was writing, this gradual development was being replaced by sudden and enormous changes in the type of machines which were being invented. These changes were to lead to a *revolution* in the way people lived.

53

Changes in the cotton industry

The change had started in the early 1700s. John Kay invented the 'flying shuttle' in 1738, which enabled a weaver to make wider pieces of cloth more quickly than before. This was followed in 1764 by the invention of the 'spinning jenny' by James Hargreaves which helped the spinner to spin cotton much more quickly than on the old spinning wheels. Janet mentions that she had a spinning jenny, and Tom would also have used a flying shuttle because, like almost all machines built in the hundreds of years leading to this time, the machines were small, and were powered by hand. Because of the huge demand for cloth, though, still better machines were needed.

Janet talks about Arkwright's 'spinning frame'. This was a new machine, much faster than the spinning jenny, but as Mr Tomkins told her, it was too big to fit into the house, and too heavy to be worked by hand. It needed a horse or water wheel to power it.

There was nothing new about either animals being used for power (cattle had pulled ploughs for thousands of years), or water wheels (which had powered mills to make flour for centuries). What was different about the spinning frame was that for the first time the *production of manufactured goods* relied on a machine which needed power. Remember that the houses had no gas or electricity then.

Power loom weaving at an early cotton mill

The first factories

So special buildings had to be built to house the new machines. These were the first factories. Originally they were built near fast-flowing rivers and were powered by water wheels, but soon the discovery of steam power meant factories could be built anywhere and still more powerful machines used.

These early factories were not pleasant places to work in. People had to get used to working set, very long hours, in hot, dangerous conditions. Working long hours was not in itself a problem – under the domestic system people had worked from dawn till dusk – but people found it difficult to get used to having to be at work at a fixed time, and working for six days a week. There were also a great many rules. Some are difficult

Arkwright's improved spinning machine

for us to understand. The rule about not opening windows was because the cotton thread would break if the air got too cool. The fine for being absent was because spinners who were ill were wasting the steam provided for their machine. The pay was very poor.

We have used the cotton industry as an example of the change from domestic to factory production, and it was the first industry to change. But similar changes in other industries quickly followed. Each invention led to further inventions, as for instance the need for power led to the invention of the steam engine. This led to increased use of coal, which led to hotter fires capable of smelting iron. This brought about changes in the chain-making and other iron-based industries with resulting increases in the range of metal goods and stronger, faster machines. Furthermore, as more goods, like cotton clothes, are made, so the price drops and the demand for still more goods increases, thus producing a pressure for still faster and bigger machines.

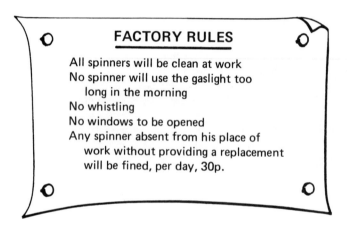

FACTORY RULES

All spinners will be clean at work
No spinner will use the gaslight too
    long in the morning
No whistling
No windows to be opened
Any spinner absent from his place of
    work without providing a replacement
    will be fined, per day, 30p.

A revolution?

When we talk about revolutions, we tend to think of armed uprisings like the French or Russian revolutions, when groups of people take over the government of a country by force. These are *political* revolutions. The Industrial Revolution was a social revolution. It too brought about great changes in the way people lived, but rather than changing the government of the country, it changed the social conditions. It changed the way people worked and the things they could buy. And it was not brought about by fighting. There was some fighting, particularly when people tried to stop the new machines threatening their old jobs, or wanted to change the very poor conditions, but this fighting did not *cause* the changes. It is called a revolution because it happened so quickly and so dramatically. In 1750 virtually everyone either lived in the country working on the land, or like Janet and Tom as domestic workers. By 1850 three quarters of the population lived in towns and cities, and half the workforce was employed in factories.

And the enormous increase in the country's wealth (the amount of goods and services produced in the country) which industrialization brought during this time, not only vastly increased the amount and type of goods which ordinary people were able to buy, but also directly led to Britain's new position as the wealthiest and most powerful country in the world — ruling three quarters of the world's population, and two thirds of its surface area.

Questions

1   Why were Janet and Tom called 'domestic workers'?

2   What can you learn from Janet's letter about:
   a) The age at which children were expected to 'pay their way'
   b) The age at which children were considered adult?

3   Why was Tom thinking of working on the canal?

4   What were the changes taking place in cotton making at the time Janet was writing?

5   Why did Janet think her friend would like the changes?

6   Why did the new machine have to be housed in factories?

7   Imagine you are Mary (or her husband Bill) writing back to Janet (or Tom). You work in one of the new factories. Describe your life and how it has changed from what you did before. What is one of your days like?

Inventors and inventions

You have seen how the Industrial Revolution came about because of new types of machinery invented at the time. But this is not the whole story. These inventions on their own could not have had such an effect. Like any invention, they had to come at the right time.

Example of an invention at the wrong time

Leonardo da Vinci 'invented' a helicopter in Italy in 1485. That is to say he made drawings of a machine which might just have worked had he had an engine to power it. But since the discovery of the petrol engine was still four centuries away in the future, his invention came to nothing.

Richard Arkwright's spinning machine came at the right time though. Because of improvements in medicine and agriculture people were healthier and were living longer, and the population was growing. (It doubled between 1750 and 1850, and doubled again between then and 1900.) There was therefore an increasing demand for clothes. And

Arkwright's machine used a water wheel (already in existence) to power it. Once such machines are in use, however, new and better ways of powering them (like steam) become inventions at the right time too. And once you have steam, you can then invent machines that would not work without steam power, like locomotives.

All the inventions on these pages happened in Britain during the Industrial Revolution, and all contributed to the growth of factories and modern industries as they are now.

James Watt — steam power

It is said that James Watt got the idea of the steam engine by watching the stream of steam from the spout of a boiling kettle. This is most unlikely,

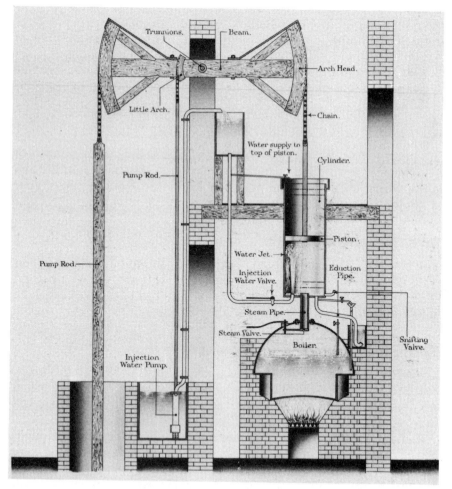

Newcomen's steam pumping engine 1712

This diagram shows a typical atmospheric pumping engine, as made by Newcomen, in section, with the piston in the middle of the downward or working stroke. Steam is generated at atmospheric pressure in the boiler and fills the cylinder during the upward stroke of the piston. The steam valve is then closed and the steam is condensed by a jet of cold water causing a vacuum under the piston. The atmospheric pressure acting on the top of the piston forces it down, hence the name 'atmospheric' engine, and this constitutes the working stroke. The piston is raised again by the overbalancing weight of the pump-rods.

because a man called **Thomas Newcomen** had already used the principle of steam power in his *beam engine* which was a pump driven by steam used to clear the water out of mines. What Watt did was to link steam power to a piston and crank, so that steam could turn an axle, and therefore a machine.

The world's first steam engine was built in 1769.

As the Industrial Revolution gathered pace, iron became increasingly important, because of its strength in withstanding the forces in steam driven machines. Once methods of working with iron had improved, all sorts of common articles, from beds to fire grates, could be made with the same techniques.

Foundry and mill at Broseley

Abraham Darby

He perfected the process of producing *iron* using coal in 1709. Iron ore is found in many parts of Britain, but to be turned into useful metal, the ore has to be smelted, or heated to a molten state to separate the iron from its ore. This had been done for hundreds of years by using charcoal to heat the ore. Charcoal is obtained by half-burning wood, and smelting iron with charcoal takes a long time and a great deal of wood. Coal, or coke, will produce far more heat than charcoal and can be used on a larger scale. Darby's factory at Coalbrookdale in Shropshire produced large quantities of iron using the new process, building amongst other things the world's first iron bridge there in 1779.

The Ironbridge, Coalbrookdale, Shropshire

Railways and ships

The first steam locomotive was built by **Richard Trevithick** in 1804. The first railway to carry passengers was built between Stockton and Darlington in 1825, and used **George Stevenson**'s engine 'Locomotion'. The famous 'Rocket' was built in 1830 and powered the first 'proper' railway between Liverpool and Manchester. Railways soon replaced the canals, built over the previous century, as the major way of moving goods around the country from producer to customer. Good transport is essential in an industrial country and the railway network spread quickly. Famous among the railway engineers is **Isambard Kingdom Brunel**, who as well as his work on railways built the first steam powered ship to cross the Atlantic in 1845 (the 'Great Britain'). The first iron ship was built in

1818 by the Scot **Thomas Watson**. The iron ships were stronger than wooden ships and had more room inside for cargo, but also needed more power — steam instead of sail. The building of iron ships and the railways greatly increased the demand for iron and later steel during the 19th century.

Agriculture

Changes in food production were vital, leading as they did to the ability to support an increasing population in the industrial towns and cities. **Robert Ransome** invented the metal plough in 1785, and **Jethro Tull** invented the seed drill (for the more efficient sowing of seed) in the 1730s. **Joseph Bryce** built a mechanical reaper (for harvesting crops) in 1799. The biggest advance in agriculture was not an invention at all though.

Cuguot's locomotive

It was a series of laws passed in the late 1700s called the 'Enclosure Acts'. These led to farm land being laid out in large fields (instead of the old small strips) enclosed by fences or hedges. Thus the new machinery could be used and previously wasted land brought under cultivation. Fewer people were needed on the land, and many moved to the cities to work in factories.

Jethro Tull's seed drill

Coal

Coal has been used as a fuel for thousands of years, but it is most useful in industrial processes in the form of coke. Abraham Darby discovered how to change coal to coke, and used the process in his ironworks. The subsequent demand for coal and coke to produce iron and steam was satisfied by various developments in mining. In 1816 **Sir Humphrey Davy** invented his famous safety lamp in which the light is surrounded by gauze. The gauze allows air in to keep the lamp alight, but prevents the flame setting fire to the explosive gases found underground. Thomas Newcomen had invented his beam engine to pump water out of mine shafts, thereby allowing deep mining, in 1705, and in 1868 **James Anderton** built a machine to cut the coal off the coal face. It was a revolving cutter very similar to the ones in use today, although whereas his was powered by steam, modern ones use electricity.

Gas

Natural gas has been used for many centuries, but artificial gas (made from coal) was not discovered until the 1600s. It was first used to light a factory in 1798, by **William Murdock**, replacing the feeble and smelly oil lamps, and was brought to the streets of London in 1813. Gas lighting was not very efficient, however, until a German, **Robert von Bunsen**, found a way of mixing air with the gas before it was burnt, in 1855. His invention can still be seen in the bunsen burner. Since then, gas has been used continuously for heating, though not for lighting since the invention of electric power at the turn of the twentieth century. Coal gas was replaced in Britain by natural gas from the North Sea during the 1960s.

A Davy lamp   A Bunsen burner

Medicine

Various developments in medicine and public health led to a smaller number of babies dying in infancy, and fewer older children and adults dying from disease. Examples of these are the opening of the London drainage system to sewage in 1815, and the discovery in 1865 of the use of antiseptics to combat infection by **Joseph Lister**.

Summary

All the discoveries and inventions listed above happened between about 1710 and 1850, and together greatly improved the type and quantity of goods produced, or the methods of producing them. This use of inventions to improve the production of goods is called *technology*. People argue about what the most important cause of this huge advance in technology was.

Was it the inventiveness of pioneers like Darby, Arkwright and Brunel?
Was it the improvements in farming and health which caused the population to grow so quickly and demand more goods?
Was it the chance that Britain happens to have a lot of coal and iron ore?
Was it the discovery of steam power?

It is best to think of it as a combination of all these factors all happening together and helping each other − it is a question of 'inventions at the right time'.

More recent inventions

Electricity

The light bulb was invented separately by **Joseph Swan** in England, and **Thomas Edison** in USA in 1879, and the electric generator in 1867, but electricity did not come into general use in Britain until 1900. Part of the reason was that industry was already well supplied with coal and gas. It was only with the building of the London Underground that its advantages became clear, and since then we have come to rely on electricity more and more, with such inventions as the telephone, radio and television. It is worth noting that with the exception of hydro-electricity, all our power stations still use steam to drive their different generators, although the steam is produced in several ways.

Oil

Oil has long been used for lighting, and for the lubrication of the new metal machines since 1700. There was a thriving industry extracting oil and oil shale rocks in West Lothian, Scotland, throughout the 19th century. Although petrol had been known about for some time, no use was found for it until the invention of the internal combustion engine in Austria in 1876. A cheaper source of oil (and hence petrol) than oil shale was found with the drilling of the first oil well in Texas in 1870, and these two developments together led to the first motor cars, built by Benz and Daimler in 1885 and 1886. Cars did not become reliable or popular until the 20th century, but were soon to challenge the railways. It was the internal combustion engine too, which led to the invention of the aeroplane by the Wright brothers in 1903, 418 years after da Vinci's 'invention at the wrong time'.

What have you discovered?

1   Divide your page into columns like this:

Date	Industrial processes	Power sources and machines	Medicine and agriculture	Other devices

Now go through all the inventions and discoveries we have listed in this section between 1700 and 1875 and write them in the appropriate column in *chronological* order (ie put the earliest first). For example Abraham Darby first smelted iron using coke in 1709. So 1709 would go in the first column, and since smelting is an industrial process, you would write 'Darby smelted iron using coke' in the second column.

2   *'The pioneers'*. Write a sentence about each of these particularly significant inventors or pioneers: Abraham Darby, Richard Arkwright, James Watt, Isambard Kingdom Brunel, Richard Trevithick.

3 What does 'technology' mean?

4 Which do you think is the *single most important* invention we have listed? Why this one?

5 Can you find out the dates of these more recent 'firsts': first person in space, first nuclear power station, first jet aircraft, first digital computer.

Different types of industry

There are many thousands of different firms in Britain. Some employ tens of thousands of workers, others employ only one or two. Some are household names, others have not been heard of outside their immediate town, or even road. Some big firms you will not have heard of because they only sell goods to other firms, and not to the public. Some firms use a great deal of machinery, other very little. Some firms only make goods, others only retail them; a few do both. Because of all these differences it is useful to try and sort firms out, or classify them, by looking at the types of things they do.

ARC's Batts Combe Quarry, Frome, Somerset

Primary industry

All raw materials started out initially as natural products which were grown or dug out of the land or sea. The firms which grow them or dig them out are called *primary* firms, and make up our primary industry.

Primary means the first stage (like primary schools are the first stage in education), and primary industry deals with the *first stage* in the production of goods.

Examples of primary industry are *farming, fishing, forestry, mining, quarrying* and the *oil industry*. In all of these a natural product is either grown, harvested, or extracted from the earth or sea. Among our biggest primary firms are the Forestry Commission, the National Coal Board and British Petroleum (BP), but there are also many smaller firms involved in this work. Many of them you will never hear of because they only sell raw materials, like limestone, leather, silicon and aluminium to other firms for these firms to process and so turn into manufactured goods.

Manufacturing industry

Manufacturing industry is the next stage in production, and is sometimes called *secondary industry*. A manufacturing firm takes a number of raw materials (often from primary firms) and turns them through processing into finished products. Whereas primary industry can be found at mines, farms and oil wells, manufacturing industry takes place in factories.

Virtually all the products we buy in shops, with the exception of fresh food, were produced by manufacturing firms. Major British manufacturers include British Leyland, Tube Investments (TI – who make Creda, Russell Hobbs and Raleigh products), Guest Keen and Nettlefolds (GKN – who make many car components among other things), Lucas and British Aerospace. Major foreign manufacturers of whom you may have heard include Datsun, IBM (who make computers) and Sony.

Service industry

A great many firms do not actually make anything. They either transport people or goods, sell goods, provide financial services like banking and insurance, provide education and health services, or provide personal services like catering, hairdressing, window cleaning and the like. All these firms are classed as *service industry* because they provide services to other firms or members of the public. In addition the government and local authorities provide services and are therefore included in Service Industry, although they are not really firms. Because these firms provide the final, or third stage in the production of goods, the stage of bringing goods from the factory to the shop and customer they are sometimes called *tertiary* industry.

Where people work

This is very different from the picture at the beginning of the century,

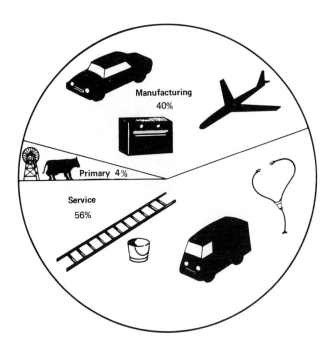

when 10% of the workforce worked in mining (a primary industry) alone. At that time far more people than today worked in manufacturing industry as well. The trend has been for more and more of the population to be employed in service industry as the years have gone by, and comparatively fewer in primary and manufacturing industry. This trend is still continuing.

Why so many in service industries?

This is typical of the richer industrial countries. As industry becomes more efficient and productive, fewer people are required to produce the same amount of goods. Because less people are employed, but are producing just as much, their pay goes up and they can afford to spend it on services as well as goods. This increased demand for services requires more people to provide them – the people who are no longer needed in manufacturing. Remember that the *wealth* of a country includes the value of the services it provides as well as the goods it makes. However without manufacturing industry to produce the wealth initially in the form of goods, there would be no money to provide any services at all.

Because so many people work in service industries, we will break this down into different sections:

You will be able to count up and see that fourteen million people work in service industries, out of a total workforce of about twenty-five million people. There are fifty-six million people living in Britain, the thirty-one million who are not in employment being roughly equally divided

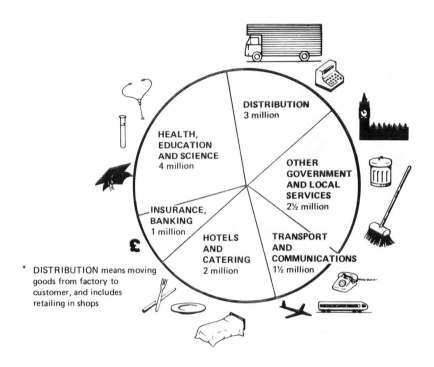

DISTRIBUTION
3 million

HEALTH,
EDUCATION
AND SCIENCE
4 million

OTHER
GOVERNMENT
AND LOCAL
SERVICES
2½ million

INSURANCE,
BANKING
1 million

HOTELS
AND
CATERING
2 million

TRANSPORT
AND
COMMUNICATIONS
1½ million

* DISTRIBUTION means moving
goods from factory to
customer, and includes
retailing in shops

between children at school and below age five, mothers who are at home bringing up children, and people who have retired from work due to age or ill health.

Types of employers

Nearly seven people out of every ten work for a private firm. This means a firm which has shareholders who have either invested their money in the firm, or have bought shares in the firm off previous shareholders. Many of the shareholders, who actually own the firm, are members of the public, but some shares are owned by trade unions, pension funds or the government. Firms whose shares can be bought and sold at The Stock Exchange by members of the public are called *public companies.*

Some firms are completely owned by the government, and have no other shareholders. These are called *nationalized industries* in the case of firms which were once private but which for one reason or another the government has now taken over, or *public corporations* in the case of the few organizations the government started from scratch. Some firms were *nationalized* (bought by the government) because they could no longer afford the massive sums needed to invest in modern machinery without government help. Examples are British Rail and the National Coal Board. Others, like British Leyland, were nationalized because they went bankrupt and the government did not want them to close down and therefore cause a lot of unemployment. A third group of firms were

68

nationalized because the government at the time thought they ought to be owned by everyone (ie the government) rather than by individual people. British Steel falls into this group. Examples of public corporations are The Post Office and the BBC. One worker in twelve is employed by a nationalized industry or public corporation.

In addition, 20% of the workforce (one worker in five) is employed by the government directly (the civil service), or by the local authorities, the health boards or the armed forces.

And one worker in fourteen is *self-employed* — that is they work on their own account, perhaps as a window cleaner or builder, and are not employed by anyone.

Private sector 72%		Public sector 28%	
Private firms (including public companies) 65%	Self-employed 7%	Nationalised industries 8%	Govt, local authorities etc 20%

Questions

1 Write down *definitions* (what they mean) of primary, manufacturing and service industry.

2 Draw *three* columns across your page, headed 'primary', 'manufacturing' and 'service'.
   a) Put each of these activities in the correct column: herring fishing, shoemaking, coal mining, window cleaning, making ball-points pens, drilling for oil, teaching, making cars and nursing.
   b) And now do the same for each of these firms or organizations: Shell, Pye, the Forestry Commission, the National Health Service, Ford, Marks and Spencer, British Airways.

3 Is the number of people employed in service industries getting bigger or smaller? Why?

4 Look at the *five* headings (excluding the government) which we gave for service industry. Can you name two firms or other organizations under each heading?

5 Are more people in Britain employed, or not employed? What are those who are not employed doing?

6 Draw a pie chart showing the proportions of the workforce employed by private firms, self-employed, working for nationalized industries and public corporations, and working for the government and local authorities.

We have divided firms into different types of industry, but it is important to remember that these different types of industry do not work in isolation of each other. Quite the opposite — they depend on each other. Manufacturing industry depends on Primary industry to provide it with raw materials. Distribution (a Service industry) depends on Manufacturing or Primary industry to give it something to distribute. And all types of industry depend on various Service industries to keep them running, like banking, insurance, retailing and transport. These commercial services are called *Commerce*. It is said that Commerce 'oils the wheels on which industry runs'. Without Commerce, industry would quickly 'seize up'.

Within each type of industry too, firms depend on each other. Let us look more closely at Manufacturing industry. We can divide it up into different sections, just as we did for Service industry.

Engineering — This includes those firms concerned with *metal* or *machinery*.

Construction — The firms involved in *building*.

Food — Those firms dealing with the processing, packing and freezing of fresh food.

Science — The firms which work with chemicals, or oil and oil related products.

All of these depend on Primary industry of one type or another. Engineering and Construction depend on minerals and timber; Science on chemicals and oil extracted from the earth; and Food on agriculture and fishing.

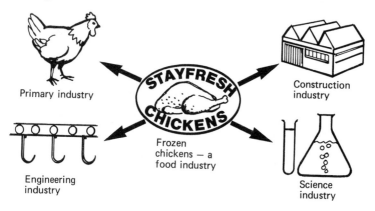

Primary industry

Construction industry

Engineering industry

Frozen chickens — a food industry

Science industry

But they also depend on each other. A factory building cars is an example of the engineering industry. But the work takes place in a factory building (Construction), using, among other things, paint (Science), and powered by oil (petro-chemicals — a Science industry).

Similarly, a factory producing frozen chickens is an example of the food industry. Yet the factory uses machinery (engineering), chemicals (science) and is housed in a building (construction).

The engineering industry

In particular, all industries depend on machinery, and therefore on the engineering industry. Some industries have their own special branches of engineering, concerned with their own particular machines.

Agricultural engineering

Marine engineering

Aeronautical engineering

Refrigeration engineering

Other branches of the engineering industry are more general. There are three main general branches:

Mechanical engineering – dealing with moving machinery. The motor industry is an example of mechanical engineering, hence the word 'mechanic'.

Electrical engineering – dealing with machinery powered by electricity. This covers everything from washing machines to computers.

Civil engineering – dealing with the building of roads and bridges, harbours and dams, and such like.

The construction industry

Similarly, most industries take place in a building and therefore depend on the construction industry. The construction industry too can be divided into different branches, according to the type of building work being undertaken:

Trowel trades, concerned with plastering and brickwork

Woodworking trades

Painting and decorating

71

Construction also includes various *Building services*, and the manufacture of materials (like brick and concrete), and the selling of such materials to builders, through *Builders' merchants*.

Agriculture and food industries

Agriculture is one of the very few Primary industries the products of which go straight to the consumer, in the form of fresh fish, meat and vegetables. However more and more of our food is now being *manufactured* by the Food industry and comes to us as frozen, tinned or packaged food.

The main branches of agriculture are:

Arable farming, concerned with crops; *livestock* farming, concerned with animals; *horticulture*, which is growing crops needing special care, like greenhouse cultivation (tomatoes, for example); *intensive* farming, which is where animals are reared in special 'factory' buildings, used commonly for chickens and eggs, and increasingly for pigs; and *orchards*, of hard fruits (like apples and pears) and soft fruits (like raspberries and strawberries).

The Food industry uses the products of agriculture as its raw materials, and can be divided into *manufacture* (frozen and canned food, baking) and *service* (hotels and restaurants, industrial catering).

Science industries

Many of the raw materials and products of the science industry now come from oil. Oil produces petrol, plastics, drugs, fertilizers and textiles like acrylic and nylon. There are many other chemicals used in industry though, and the science industry contributes to most industrial processes. Many large firms have their own laboratories.

Suggested work

1 Take *each* of the following examples, and say:
   a) what type of industry it is,
   b) what branch of that industry,
   c) what raw materials are used,
   d) whether there are any other industries on which it depends, and if so, which and
   e) whether there are any examples of the activity in your own local area.

   Example A: Manufacture of tinned tomato soup
   Example B: Manufacture of fertilizers
   Example C: Building a new motorway
   Example D: Manufacture of typewriters

2 What is *commerce*?

3 Take the *main* type of industry in which you are most interested, and describe the different branches of that industry, using examples where you can.

There is one thing that all these industries have in common. They are all involved in the *direct creation of wealth*.

The creation of wealth — profit and investment

Question: 'What is the wealth of a country?'
Answer: 'The amount of goods and services that country produces.'

We are not concerned in this book with how the wealth is divided up — who gets how much of the national 'cake' — although dividing the cake *fairly* (which does not always mean equally) is a very important job of the government.

My piece

Your piece!

We are instead concerned with the clear fact that the bigger the cake is, the more there is to divide. The amount of goods we produce in Britain is not fixed, it can increase or decrease, and it is obviously in everyone's interest to try and make it increase. We have already seen that the wealth of Britain increased enormously during the Industrial Revolution due to the *growth of industries* brought about by *technological advance*. The new inventions at the time led to far more being produced. So technological advance is one method of increasing wealth.

Technological advance

Let us look at this in the context of an individual manufacturing firm. Raw materials are *processed* into finished products, and the processes each use their own machinery. Replacing old machines with new, more efficient ones, and trying to develop new and better products are two ways a firm can increase its output — the amount of goods it produces. When a firm spends money doing either of these things it is called *investment*. Investment might take the form of simply buying new machinery. Or a large firm might employ scientists whose job is *research and development* (sometimes called R & D); that is trying to discover new and better processes or products. One of the reasons Britain's industrial growth has lagged behind that of countries like Germany and Japan since the Second World War is because those countries needed new machines to replace industries completely destroyed in the war, whereas many firms in Britain continued to use machines dating back, in some cases, well into the 19th century.

Investment costs money.

Where the money comes from

A firm's money comes from selling the goods it produces. This money has to pay for the raw materials, the labour force, the energy costs and any payments for capital items, like rent and rates for buildings, repair bills, replacement of worn out vehicles and machines, and so on. Any money left over is the firm's *profit*. If there is nothing left over, no profit, the firm will eventually go *bankrupt*, will be unable to pay its bills, and will have to close down and sack all its workers.

If there is some profit, the firm will be able to spend some of it in *investment* in new machines, research, a bigger factory, or developing new products. It is quite likely, though, that a firm will want to spend more on investment than it makes in profits, so it will need to raise some extra money. It can do this in two ways:

1 Borrowing
A firm can borrow money from a bank, or from anyone else who will lend it. The lender will expect to be paid back, of course, and will expect to get *interest* on the money. These payments will come from a firm's future profits in years to come. So a firm has to be making a profit, or has to look as if it might, before anyone will lend it money.

2 Selling shares
A firm might raise money by selling shares in itself to members of the public. Anyone buying a 'share' in the firm will give money to the firm (for investment) and in exchange will become a partowner of the firm, or *shareholder*. Each year shareholders receive part of the firm's profits, called a *dividend*. This is their return for giving the firm their money, so obviously the bigger the dividend they expect, the more likely they will be to buy a share in the firm. Shareholders are never repaid — they give money to the firm not lend it — but if they want to stop being owners, they can sell their share to someone else. The *Stock Exchange* is the place

where people sell shares to each other, and big companies have literally millions of shares, some of which change hands every day. The money people give to firms in this way is called *risk capital*: 'capital' because it goes towards capital spending, and 'risk' because the shareholders are risking their money and will lose some or all of it if the firm does badly.

There is a limit to the amount a firm can borrow since the money has to be paid back, often fairly quickly, so practically all firms, at one time or another, will have raised money by selling shares to the public. In 1981, British Petroleum (BP) raised over six hundred million pounds for new investment in this way.

A firm whose owners are members of the public is called a *public company*, although many shares nowadays are owned by pension funds, investment trusts or trade unions.

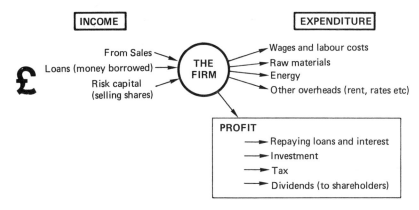

A firm that does not make any profit will not be able to borrow money or repay existing loans, not be able to invest in new machinery, and so increase the amount of goods it produces, not be able to pay dividends to shareholders, and so will be unable to raise new money for investment.

Other ways to increase wealth

Investment is very important, but it is not the only way to increase either production or profits. Profits will increase if expenditure goes down, like by the firm using less electricity. Or if the firm sells more, perhaps by more advertising or better marketing, its profits will go up. Note that putting up prices does not automatically mean a firm will make more money. Often it simply means the firm will sell fewer goods, and make even less profit. Sir Jack Cohen, who founded Tesco, once said: 'Pile it high, and sell it cheap!', meaning that if a firm sells things cheaply it will sell lots of them, and hence make a lot of profit. It certainly worked for him! It is a complicated job for a firm to fix its prices so they are high enough to make a profit, but low enough to sell the goods.

And if a firm can produce the same number of goods more cheaply than before, or more goods for the same cost, its profits will increase. This would happen if the firm persuaded its workers to work harder or more quickly, as well as by investment in more efficient machinery.

The amount of goods produced by a firm for a given number of workers is called its *productivity*. If productivity goes *up*, the firm will be making more goods than before with the same number of workers. If productivity goes *down*, the firm will be making less. Productivity can be increased by investment in more efficient machinery, or by improving the quality and work of the workforce, or by both.

The Gazelle Motor Company makes 10 cars per year for each worker.

The Elland Motor Company makes 20 cars per year for each worker.

Elland cars will be cheaper and the Elland Company will make more profit because each workers' wages are shared among 20 cars instead of 10.

Cutting down expenses = more profit
Selling more goods = more profit
Increasing productivity = more profit
More profit = more investment = more goods produced = increased wealth

All these concerns – how much to charge, how to cut down expenses, how to sell more goods, whether and how to invest, how to improve the product, how to increase productivity – are the job of the *management* of the firm.

Questions

1   Say what each of these words means (read back over the section to help you get the meanings accurate): profit; investment; productivity; risk capital.

2   Rewrite this sentence *without* using the word 'productivity': 'The productivity of the Japanese ship-building industry is greater than the productivity of the British ship-building industry.'

3　What are the main ways in which a company can raise money for investment if its profits are not large enough to pay for the investment directly?

4　If you were the manager of a firm, and you wanted to increase your firm's profits, what different ways could you go about doing this?

5　Some goods are very *sensitive* to price changes − ie if a firm puts its price up that firm will immediately lose a lot of their sales. Others are *resistant* to price change. Say whether you think each of the following is sensitive or resistant to price change, and why: petrol; gas; cigarettes; sheepskin coats; ball-point pens.

Find out

Most newspapers give lists of the share prices of at least our major companies. Can you find out what is the current price of shares in BP and Marks and Spencer? If you or your teacher has a copy of a paper giving a large list of share prices (like the *Daily Telegraph* or the *Scotsman*) your teacher will be able to help you work out what dividend shareholders in these companies got for each share last year? Can you find the share prices of any of your local companies?

Sample multiple choice questions

1　The Industrial Revolution led to
　a) the growth of cottage industries
　b) people obtaining better working conditions
　c) the beginning of the factory system
　d) the overthrow of the government of the time

2　The main types of engineering are
　a) electronics, electricity and television
　b) mechanical, electrical and civil
　c) construction, food and science
　d) marine, technical and primary

3　Introducing more efficient machinery into an industry will lead to
　a) a reduction of output
　b) increased productivity
　c) higher unit costs
　d) lower profits

4　Which of the following lists contains only service industries?
　a) insurance, banking, farming
　b) catering, mining, insurance
　c) transport, hairdressing, insurance
　d) hairdressing, education, car manufacture

5 Which of the following is involved in the direct creation of wealth?
a) a doctor
b) a lawyer
c) a factory worker
d) a shop assistant

6 Which of the following is unlikely to lead to an increase in wealth on its own?
a) investment in new machinery
b) higher productivity
c) introduction of new technology
d) increasing wages

7 An example of a Science industry is the manufacture of
a) washing machines
b) fertilizers
c) frozen chickens
d) concrete

8 Which of the following industries use the services of the engineering industry?
a) farming
b) shipbuilding
c) bread making
d) all three

9 Which of the following inventions did *not* have a great effect on the Industrial Revolution?
a) Railways
b) Electricity
c) The steam engine
d) The spinning jenny

10 Which of the following is *not* a commercial service?
a) Insurance
b) Banking
c) Retailing
d) Production

11 The Industrial Revolution led to
a) more people working in agriculture
b) more people living in towns
c) more people being employed as domestic workers
d) a drop in the population

12 Horticulture is an example of
a) the agriculture industry
b) the engineering industry
c) food manufacture
d) a science industry

13 Which of the following provides a firm with income?
    a) Wage costs
    b) Raw material costs
    c) Investment
    d) Risk Capital

14 Most working people in Britain are employed in
    a) the private sector
    b) nationalised industries
    c) manufacturing industry
    d) local authority services

15 Quarrying is an example of a
    a) primary industry
    b) manufacturing industry
    c) service industry
    d) nationalised industry

5

Housing and the local environment

Land use

We all need somewhere to live. This is probably our most important need
for and use of land. However, it is only one use of land and only one way
in which we use the *local environment*. The local environment is all the

space around us — the land, air, rivers and sea. You will be able to think of many other ways in which we use our environment; here are some of them:

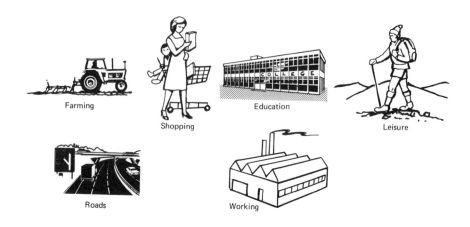

Farming

Shopping

Education

Leisure

Roads

Working

And of course there are many creatures other than ourselves who use the same environment.

A mix of building types in Sheffield

In the past, people were allowed to build whatever buildings they liked wherever they wanted to provided they owned the land. This led to towns growing up in a haphazard way, with houses interspersed among factories and warehouses. It led to shops being clustered together and surrounded by houses, with no room to build car parks, leisure areas, or wide roads. However nowadays, land use is *planned*. People cannot just build what they like, only what is suitable for the land they own.

It is the job of each local council to decide what is suitable and what is not, and people considering building have to apply to the council for *Planning Permission*. The application is in two parts: first, the applicant has to ask for *Outline* planning permission.

Outline planning permission

At this stage the person wanting to build does not submit an exact plan, only a general outline of the type of thing he or she has in mind. It might be a single house, or a whole estate, or a factory, or a school, or a yachting marina. The council will consider the application, and ask themselves three questions:

1 Is the proposed development in keeping with the other buildings already there nearby, and will it not cause undue problems for the occupants of those buildings?
2 Are the local facilities — the drains, roads and schools for example — capable of servicing the new development?
3 Is the proposed development in accordance with the general plan of land use in the area?

If the answer to all three questions is 'Yes', then outline planning permission will be granted. Let us look in more detail at what the third question means.

Zoning

In most areas, land is divided into *zones* or areas, each suitable for different uses. These will include a *Residential* zone, where the only buildings allowed will be houses, and the other buildings necessary to support the houses, like schools and local shops. There may be an *Industrial* zone, where factories and warehouses, but not houses, will be allowed. And, usually around the edge of the town, there will be a zone called the *Green belt*, where no building at all is permitted.

Because of zoning, people have to apply for permission not only to build new buildings, but also to change the use of existing ones. A man who wants to turn his garden into a trout farm will have to apply to change the use of his land from residential to agricultural.

Most towns grew up before the days of planning controls, and the zones are therefore not easy to spot. But some towns have been almost completely built since zoning came into force; these are the New Towns. One such town is Livingston, in Scotland, and from a map of the town we can clearly see how the zoning policy works.

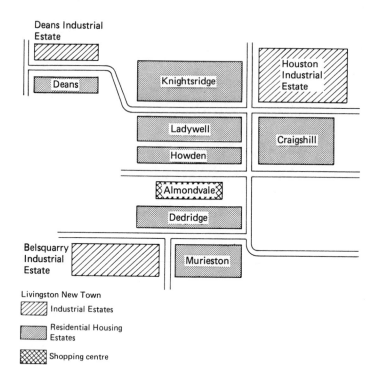

Deans Industrial Estate

Deans

Knightsridge

Houston Industrial Estate

Ladywell

Craigshill

Howden

Almondvale

Dedridge

Belsquarry Industrial Estate

Murieston

Livingston New Town

Industrial Estates

Residential Housing Estates

Shopping centre

You can see that the Industrial Estates, where all the factories are, at Deans, Houston and Belsquarry, are on the edge of the town. The areas of Knightsridge, Deans, Ladywell, Howden, Craigshill, Dedridge and Murieston are housing estates, containing only houses, small shops, schools and pubs. In the centre is Almondvale, which is the town's main shopping centre, containing all the large shops, the cinema, the police station, the bus station, and extensive car parks. Around the boundaries of the town is the Green belt, which is farming land, separating Livingston from its neighbouring towns.

If a proposed development fits into the council's zoning policy, they will consider the other two questions raised above. In all cases applications for planning permission are then advertised, and people have the chance to object to a proposal before the council finally decides on it. One example of a case where permission is almost always given is where there is a gap between two existing houses, and the developer is wanting to fill the gap with a house broadly similar to those on either side.

Suggested work

1 What is meant by 'the local environment'?

2 What will a local council consider when deciding whether to grant outline planning permission?

3 Why do you think a person applying for outline planning permission only has to submit a general outline of his or her plans, rather than a detailed proposal?

4 Look at the map of Livingston. There is a large gap between two big houses in Murieston. Mr Jones, who owns this gap site submits an application to build on it. Do you think he would get outline planning permission for any of the following plans? Say why you think he would or would not, and whether your answer is *definite*, or only a possibility:
   a) a block of flats
   b) a small factory
   c) a single house
   d) a newsagents

5 Draw a map of your own town, or the area of the city in which you live. Mark on it where the different zones are, and what the land is currently used for. You could ask your local council what its development plans are in relation to land use in the area.

6 Look in your local newspaper for any advertisements notifying applications for planning permission or change of use. Do you think they will be granted?

An industrial estate

Detailed planning permission

Once outline planning permission has been obtained for a proposed development, an application has to be made for detailed planning consent. This is because there is a great variety of possible constructions which could loosely be called a 'house', and while it might be quite suitable for a house to be built on a particular site in principle, the finished construction might well be totally unacceptable without some sort of control. It is also important to make sure that a proposed building does not adversely affect those living nearby, by cutting off their light, for example, or overshadowing one of their windows.

To obtain detailed planning permission a developer has to submit exact plans of his or her proposal, showing the size and position of the building, what it will look like, and what it will be made of.

Detailed planning permission is required for every new building, and for many alterations to the outside of existing buildings, like extensions, new windows, or porches, but minor alterations are often passed quickly and easily.

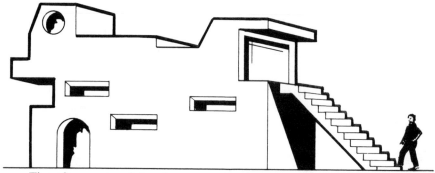

There is a great variety of
possible constructions which
could loosely be called a house.

Why bother?

People are sometimes tempted to build without asking for planning permission, particularly if they are pretty sure it would be refused, for instance when they live in a green belt. They think that the council will turn a blind eye to a 'fait accompli'. This is *not recommended*. Several such people have sorry tales to tell of being forced to demolish a new house because they built it without permission. And there is the true story of the farmer who built what he said was a new pigsty − it looked remarkably like a bungalow and even had curtains at the windows − however much he insisted it really was a pigsty, it still had to go!

Building control

Planning permission is concerned with the looks and suitability of a development. There are also controls on the internal design of a house, to make sure it is up to the standard required. These controls are contained in the *Building regulations*, and all new houses must have a certificate to show they comply with these regulations, in addition to planning permission. Internal alterations to existing houses also need a certificate, although they do not need planning permission since they do not affect the outside of the house.

The building regulations cover such items as:

Size of rooms – a bedroom, for example, must have a floor area of at least 75 square feet

Number of power points – most rooms must have at least two power points, and their height above the floor is specified

Storage Area – depending on the overall size of the house, there is a minimum amount of required cupboard or storage space

Connections to the public drains, and the internal plumbing – as an example, 'mixer' taps are not allowed when the cold water supply to the taps feeds directly off the main supply

This is the opening paragraph of the type of form used to apply for a Building warrant. The rest of the form goes on to ask detailed questions about the cost, purpose and extent of the proposed work.

CITY OF WORCESTER

THE BUILDING REGULATIONS, 1976

NOTICE OF INTENTION to:—   (*Cross out items not applicable)

*Erect a building or part of a building
        *Execute works or install fittings

*Carry out alterations or extensions
        *Make a material change of use of a building

In Accordance with Building Regulations Numbered A 10 and Schedule 2

I/WE hereby give notice that I/WE intend to carry out the work set out on this form and in accordance with the plans accompanying.

Signed . . . .   Date . . . .

---

1. Name and address of person or
   persons on whose behalf the work
   is to be carried out (In block letters
   please)

   Telephone No.

2. If signed by Agent, Name.
   Profession,
   Address.

   Telephone No.

FORM B.R./A.   Deposited Plan ....

                         Temporary Building No. ....

This notice should be addressed to:
                 The City Architect and Planning Officer,
                 1 Hylton Road,
                     WORCESTER. WR2 5JP.
                 Telephone: Worcester (0905) 23471

Listed buildings

Listed buildings are buildings of special interest, either because of their
style of architecture, or because of their historical interest. It is felt that
they should be preserved for these reasons, and so special permission is
required to make any internal or external alterations. Anyone who demo-
lishes a listed building without permission is liable to a fine or imprisonment. Similarly, an owner is not allowed to let a listed building go to 'rack
and ruin' by neglecting it, and the local council can force such an owner
to make necessary repairs to keep the building in good order.

Conservation area

Each planning authority, which usually means the local council, has to designate any areas of special architectural or historical interest in their locality as 'conservation areas'. Not every house in a conservation area is always very fine or special by itself, but the grouping of the houses together gives the whole area a special interest. An example might be the centre of a small village which has remained almost unchanged for many years. Stricter than normal controls apply to planning applications in a conservation area, and a high standard is required. Sometimes *grants* are available, however, to help house owners meet these higher standards.

Design awards

Most councils offer awards each year for house and building designs that they consider to be exceptionally good. This might be because they fit well into a conservation area, or because they are a clever way to design a particular building. It is unfortunately true that many buildings which received design awards in the past, particularly high rise buildings from the 1960's, are now regarded as horrible mistakes. Two design award winners from 1980 in West Lothian are shown here.

Restored cottages in Lion Well Wynd, Linlithgow, winner of the District Council Conservation Award 1980 — inset top left is a sketch of the commemorative plaque fitted to one of the cottages.

New Head Post Office, Bathgate, winner of the District Council Design Award 1980

Who does what?

During this chapter we have often used the word *developer* as the person making a planning application. But what is a developer?

The developer is the person who wants to *develop* a particular site: that is to put a house on it, extend a house already there, build a factory, and so on. Usually, the developer owns the site, but he or she may just have an idea which he or she wants outline permission for before buying some land. Obviously, a piece of land with outline planning permission for a house, or number of houses, is worth a great deal more than land without permission, but it would be a great risk to buy a field, say, in the hopes that you might get permission to build some houses. The difference really is colossal. A field without planning permission might be worth £3000, whereas with planning permission for an estate of houses it could be worth £100 000, or even more.

Once the developer has outline planning permission, or in a case such as a house extension where it would not be needed, he or she will consult an *architect*. The architect knows how to draw up plans for the work, what materials to use for different parts of the building, what the finished building will look like, and so on. These architect's plans will be used by the developer when applying for detailed planning permission and a building warrant.

Once detailed permission and a warrant have been obtained, the developer will choose a builder whose job it is actually to build the house or whatever in accordance with the plans.

Here is a plan of the sequence of events:

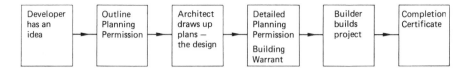

| Developer has an idea | Outline Planning Permission | Architect draws up plans — the design | Detailed Planning Permission Building Warrant | Builder builds project | Completion Certificate |

With minor works, like house extensions, or loft conversions (when a loft is floored to make an extra room) some firms will offer to do all this.

Suggested work

1 What are Building Control regulations?

2 What is a Building warrant?

3 What is a listed building? Can you find an example of a listed building near where you live?

4 Look at the two examples of design award winners. Why do you think these buildings received awards?

5 If a building firm spotted a field which they thought would be a good spot for a housing estate, would they try and buy the land before or after obtaining outline or detailed planning permission. Why?

6 What is a completion certificate?

Aesthetics

Aesthetics means designing a building, or anything else for that matter, which not only looks good, but works well too. We often use the word *functional* if something works well. So something with aesthetic properties is both functional and pleasing to look at.

It is not always easy to do both in the same design. A chair might look very pleasing, but be uncomfortable or give no back support. A family saloon car must be designed to take at least two adults and three children, together with their luggage. However nice it looks, it is no good if the boot will not take a suitcase. And of course, nothing can be functional if it is *unsafe*.

Usually a design is a *compromise* between good looks and function. Sometimes one is more important than the other. With a piece of machinery in a factory the function is much more important than the looks. With a carpet, both are important. With a piece of jewellery, the looks are more important, in fact without the right looks it would have no function at all.

Often we just 'know' what looks good without knowing why, and sometimes there is in fact no reason. Some fashions, like in clothes, seem to change from year to year, and what looks fine in 1978 looks totally wrong in 1982. There are some guidelines, though, which help things to look 'right'.

a) Things should fit in with their surroundings. Anything which is very different from local practice will probably look odd.

b) All the parts should go together with each other. That is why some estate cars look a bit ungainly. They are really saloon car designs which have had an estate back stuck on to them. Another example of this is in garden walls. A garden wall should be built of the same material as the house it surrounds, or failing this, of a local stone. If it is, it will suit both the house and the local area, and therefore look pleasing to the eye.

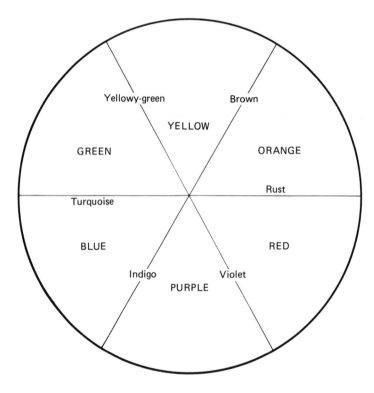

c) Colours are very important. Some colours go together, others do not. We use the word *harmonise* to describe going together. Some colours, although they do not harmonise, stand out from each other in an attractive, eye-catching way. Such colours are said to *contrast*.

Look at the colour wheel. Those colours next door to each other in the wheel harmonise – they go well together. So purple and red harmonise, as do blue and green. However red and blue do not look good together, and neither do orange and green. Contrasting colours are opposite to each other in the wheel: red contrasts with green, purple with yellow, and so on. Only a little bit of a contrasting colour should be used, but then can look very pleasing. An orange tin opener would look attractive with a blue handle, for example, but would look not nearly as nice with a green one.

Colours can also change the apparent size of a room. Dark walls make a room look smaller, and a dark ceiling makes the ceiling look lower. On the other hand light colours tend to increase space. And people often associate red colours with warmth, and blue colours with coolness. If you have a small, cold bathroom, do not paint it dark blue!

d) The overall shape of something can make it look pleasing or otherwise. In general things should not be too tall or thin, or too short and wide. And for some objects, an *axis of symmetry* adds to the design. This means that you could draw an imaginary line through the object, and the shape of the object on one side of the line would be 'mirrored' on the other side. In the star shape shown below, the line X − X makes an axis of symmetry, but the line Y − Y does not.

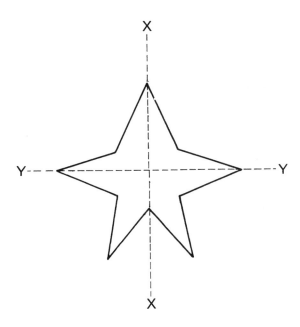

Economy

As well as *function* and *pleasing looks*, a designer also has to consider *cost*. There is no point in designing a very attractive and highly functional object which no one can afford to buy. With some objects the cost is more important than with others. With a Rolls Royce, cost definitely takes third place after looks and function, whereas with a Mini Metro cost is far more important if the makers want to sell their cars. So the designers of the Mini Metro will have had to give up some of their aesthetic considerations on the grounds of economy.

Suggested work

1   What does 'aesthetics' mean?

2   Can you list five items where the function of the item is clearly more important than the looks? And five where the opposite is true?

3   Why is it probably 'wrong' to build a garden wall out of brick around a stone-built house?

4   Suggest a colour scheme, with reasons, for a very large, but low-ceilinged sitting room with a rust coloured carpet. What colours would you choose for the walls, ceiling and woodwork?
    You should be able to get hold of painting colour charts from your local suppliers. How do the manufacturers suggest you mix their colours?

5   How many axes of symmetry does an oval have? And a six pointed star?

Types of buildings

There is a great variety of buildings in any town. Some are large, some small, some old, and some new. They vary according to their *purpose*. A factory, a shop, a college and a house all look very different. Many, however, are instantly recognisable because their design is very much influenced by their *function*. So much so, that if you went into a shop or school built 150 or even 500 years ago, you would immediately know what it was.

Houses, however, although they too are all built for the same function − that of living in − vary enormously. Even those built at roughly the same time can share very little in common with one another. Let us look at the main different types of house one finds.

a) *Flats*   A flat is one *unit* of a larger building, and has other units occupied by other families either above, or below, or both. By effectively stacking houses up on top of each other, a lot of people can be housed on a small amount of land. Flats tend to be common, therefore, where land is very expensive, or in short supply. Some people like living in flats, but there are many disadvantages − where do the children play? What do you do when the lifts break down?

Semi-detached houses

A row of terraced houses

b) *Terraced houses* A terraced house is also one unit of a larger building, but in this case the houses are side by side. The side walls of one house also form the side walls of the houses next door. Because there is no space between the houses, terraced houses make economical use of land and are thus comparatively cheap. The house at the end of the row, which has only one 'common' wall, is usually called an *end terrace*.

c) *Semi-detached houses (or 'semis')* A semi-detached house is joined on to only one other house. It therefore has space on one side, but not the other.

d) *Detached houses* A detached house stands in its own ground and is not attached to any other houses. Although it might be identical to a semi-detached house on the same estate it will be more expensive to build because it has no 'common' walls and will use more land, having space on both sides.

A detached house

In general, a detached house is thought to be best. The occupants can make as much noise as they like without disturbing neighbours through the 'common' wall, and there will be slightly more garden than in an equivalent semi-detached or terraced house. The house itself will not necessarily be bigger, of course. Some Victorian semi-detached and terraced houses have many more rooms than modern detached houses, and there is a growing number of 'small' (say two bedroomed) detached houses being built nowadays. Some developers try to get the advantages of detached houses without the expense by joining two houses together along the walls of their garages. Such houses are called 'link-detached'.

Houses also vary according to how, and of what, they are built. This might be red or coloured brick; grey or cotswold stone; rendered (covered in little pebbles – pebbledash, or pieces of shell); wood; or pre-cast concrete sections. There might be a local building material (red-brick or a type of stone), and the roofs might be flat or sloping, tiled or slate.

Houses have changed a lot over the years, as you will see if you look at houses of different ages in your local area. As land has got more expensive gardens have got much smaller, and houses have been designed to fit more rooms into a smaller space. This has been partly achieved by wasting less space inside the house in little nooks and crannies, but mostly it has led to smaller rooms, in many modern houses down to the minimum sizes allowed in the building regulations. On the other hand, more storage space (like fitted wardrobes) is built into newer houses, kitchens and bathrooms are much better equipped, and garages and central heating are becoming more common.

Buy or rent

There are two ways of getting a house – buying and renting. Most people who rent houses rent them from a local council, or in the new towns from the Development Corporation, but it is also possible to rent from a Housing Association or from a private landlord. Housing Associations are non-profit-making organizations set up to help provide houses in areas of shortage. Private landlords/landladies are people who for one reason or another have houses they are not living in which they rent out to make money. Not all private landlords/landladies make a living from their houses, they might be servicemen or women, or other people who have to go abroad for a year or two, who do not want to leave their houses empty meantime.

Renting from a local council is much cheaper than renting from a private landlord because the rent is *subsidised* by the council. (That is the council pays part of the rent themselves.) People wishing to rent a council house have to fill in an application form and go on the council's 'waiting list'. The length of the waiting list depends on how many people want council houses in a particular area, and it can be very long indeed. Priority is given to certain applicants, however, particularly those without a home already, those with young children, those who have to move (from a flat perhaps) for health reasons, and those who have moved to the area to work for the council itself. Renting a council house is possible once you are sixteen, but it is unlikely that a council will have

BELLSQUARRY'S VILLAGE

217 Caldero Road

Detached stone-built Cottage, situated in quiet cul-de-sac village, consisting of lounge, 3 bedrooms, kitchen and bathroom. Full gas-fired central heating. Roof insulated. Timber garages.

Rateable value, £296.

On view Sat. and Sun. 2-4 p.m., or phone Livingstone 410749.

Offers over £25,000.

CRAXTONS, SSC,
156 GEORGE STREET,
EDINBURGH,
031-225-60251

36998AB

BELLSQUARRY'S VILLAGE

Attractive end-terraced Cottage, beautiful location with nice open view at front and side. Close to shoping centre and Edinburgh. Tiled entrance hall, livingroom, kitchen with extractor fan, wood panel, Delft tiles, new floor, bathroom suite with shower, wide corridor with 2 large storage cupboards, 3 bedrooms, rear hall, large storage space. Nice big garden with barbecue area. Fitted carpets in bedrooms and corridor. Full solid fuel central heating. Garage, coal bin and extras. Nice neighbourhood.

Offers over £25,000.

For viewing telephone Livingstone 2410755.

158577Z

BROXBURN

148 Parkwood Gardens
FIXED PRICE, £27,500

Very attractive Villa in highly desirable estate, comprising lounge/diningroom, fully-fitted kitchen with solid wood cupboard units, 3 bedrooms, bathroom with coloured suite, hall. Extended garage. Well laid-out and stocked garden front and rear. Full gas central heating. Many extras included, e.g., all fitted carpets, all curtains, etc.

Rateable value, £322.

Viewing 7-9 weekday evenings, 2-4 Saturday and Sunday, or telephone Broxburn 8546212.

Further particulars from and offers to:

E. S. TATE

277489X

EAST CALDERON

934 Overton Crescent

East Calderon is a thriving rural community just 20 mins. from Edinburgh. This detached Villa on a good corner site comprises 4/5 well proportioned apartments, all in good order throughout, providing ideal family accommodation. Cavity wall and loft insulation: full double glazing and full gas central heating – the perfect combination for economy. Has to be seen to be excellent value for money at the fixed price of £27,000.

Viewing Thurs. 7-8 p.m., Sun 2-4 p.m. or contact Agents.

Building society mortgage readily available. Further particulars from and offers to:

Stuartson Wyse Ogilvie
2111A, GEORGE RD
EDINBURGH 0031-225 5286

E5741 1D

LINLITHGOW

4 Carmelawson

Forming part of a select Walker Homes development on the southern boundary of the town close to Beecraigs Country Park, this superior 4-bedroomed detached Villa offers generous family accommodation, all well maintained and tastefully decorated. Also comprising entrance hall, large open-plan lounge/dining-room, kitchen, utility room, bathroom, additional toilet. Garage and garden. Full gas central heating and double glazing throughout.

Rateable value, £478.

To view telephone Linlithgow 48212.

Offers over £44,000.

Carpets by private negotiation.

Caesar & Howice
═ SOLICITORS ═
27-29 George Rd, Bathgate,
Tel: Bathgate 552115

847835V

LIVINGSTONE

40 Braid Green
FIXED PRICE, £24,000
IMMEDIATE ENTRY

Attractive semi-detached modern Villa. Lounge/dining-room, 3 bedrooms, fitted kitchen, bathroom and garage. Gas central heating, double glazing. Fitted carpets and curtains throughout.

Rateable value, £350. To view tel. 0689 61790. Further particulars from:

Saitken Kinnear & CoWS
35-37 Queen Ave, Edinburgh
EH2 1LQ Tel. 031-225 29149

ESRC
24343K

ROSLIN

13 Corston Park
FIXED PRICE, '11,500

Pleasantly situated third floor flat in centre of town. Sitting Room/Kitchen, bedroom, small bathroom. Ideal first time buyer. Well modernised.

Rateable value, £125.

Viewing weekdays 7-9 pm, weekends 2-4 pm, or phone 58931376 or after 6 pm 031-66133932.

Offers to:
LOUISE MARUS, Solicitor,
114 GLOUCESTER PLACE,
EDINBURGH,
Tel. 031-225 74399

812448U

houses available for young, single people.

There are alternatives to renting a whole house; it is possible to share a house, or flat, with other people, or to rent a room in someone else's house. A room on its own is commonly called a 'bed-sit' (the room is both bedroom and sitting room), or 'digs' if some meals are provided as well. In big cities there are usually hostels, like those run by the YMCA or YWCA, which provide rooms for single people.

Buying a house

More than half the people in Britain live in houses they have *bought*. Buying a house has certain advantages over renting:

a) There is no waiting list. You choose a house you like in the area where you want to live, buy it, and move in.
b) You are free to decorate your house, inside and out, just as you please. Subject to planning permission and building regulations you can alter your house, extend it, improve it, just as you like.
c) There is no rent to pay, and when you die you can pass on the house, or its value, to your children.

The advantages of renting are that you get your house maintained and repaired for you at no cost, and of course you do not have to buy it in the first place. And buying a house is a very expensive business. Look at these advertisements for houses up for sale. Read the descriptions of the houses and look at their price. (NB A *villa* just means a house with an upstairs, as opposed to a *bungalow*; a *cottage* is an older type of house.)
You will see there is not much under £20 000. Can you find any?

The cheapest house on the page is actually the flat in Roslin for £11 500 which contains a sitting room and kitchen combined, a bedroom, and a small bathroom. Yet there are very few people, particularly young couples, who can afford even this much money, let alone the £24 000 the three bedroomed semi-detached house in the advertisement above costs. So how do people manage to buy themselves a house? The answer is that they *borrow* the money, paying it back over a long time, usually 25 years.

There are three main sources of borrowing the money to buy a house – the local council, a bank, or a building society. Anyone wishing to buy a house should go to all three.

Building societies

You will have heard of the Halifax, Abbey National and Leeds Building Societies. Like all other building societies they were set up to help people buy their own homes. They work by taking money in from *savers*, or investors, and then lending this money to house buyers. The money they lend to a buyer is called a *mortgage*. In general, the building societies will lend up to two and a half times a person's yearly income. So a person

98

A bank branch

earning £100 a week, or £5200 a year, will be able to borrow £13 000. They usually expect a buyer to have saved some of the price of the house themselves – this is called the *deposit*. A common amount they look for is 10% of the price, and they will then give a 90% mortgage to cover the rest. Sometimes a full 100% mortgage is possible (look at the Roslin advertisement again).

Building societies are good places to save money; money can be paid in and taken out at will, and the societies pay *interest* on the money saved up with them. They pay this interest by charging interest to their borrowers, however. The interest varies from time to time, and is added to the amount a borrower repays on his mortgage each month. The table shows the approximate amount a person will have to pay each month over 25 years to pay back different mortgages when the interest rate is 13%. (The interest paid is actually a lot less than 13% because borrowers get *tax relief* on their mortgage interest. The figures in the table take this into account.)

Amount of mortgage	Monthly payment
£25 000	£210
£20 000	£168
£15 000	£126
£10 000	£84
£5 000	£42

So even the small flat in Roslin will cost the buyer £90 a month and the three bedroomed semi-detached would cost £200, or nearly £50 a week. This is perhaps double what an equivalent council house would cost to rent.

The good news

However, unlike a council house rent which goes up each year usually, a mortgage payment is more or less fixed for the 25 years. Interest rates may go up or down, but the amount will not increase yearly. So in only five to ten years the mortgage payment will actually be less than the equivalent council rent, and will go on being less until it disappears altogether when the loan is repaid.

Not only that, but the value of the house will probably go up at the same time. The Roslin flat could well be worth £25 000 in seven years time, and if the person who buys it decides then to move to a bigger house, he or she will be able to pay back the £11 500 borrowed and have £13 500 left over to put towards a new house.

Too good to be true?

Not at all. People who buy their own house, and anyone over 18 can get a

100

mortgage, certainly have to scrimp and save at first, but they are rarely disappointed in the long run.

As we said earlier, banks will also lend money for house buying, and their mortgages work very like building society ones. The local council is slightly different. It is now a legal right for anyone renting a council house to buy that house from the council, and if they have been in the house some time, they will get a discount of up to 50% off the price. However it may be that they cannot get a mortgage from a building society or bank. In this case the council *must* lend them the money itself, but sometimes charges slightly more interest. It is always worth asking the council, but it is probably cheaper to borrow from the other two sources if you can.

Suggested work

1   What is the difference between a 'terraced' and a 'detached' house?

2   Is it always true that a detached house is bigger than a semi-detached?

3   Can you think of any reasons why someone would *want* to live in a flat?

4   Look round your local area. Can you divide the streets up into the types and age of the houses? Is there a local stone?

5   What are the advantages of renting a house over buying one?

6   What are the advantages of buying a house rather than renting?

7   Look in your local paper at the house advertisements. How much would it cost to buy a small house? A three bedroomed house?

8   You will notice that the flat we talked about in Roslin has been 'modernised'. What does this mean? A good way to buy a house cheaply is to buy one that has not been modernised. Are there any for sale like that in your local paper? What do they cost? Grants are available to help people make certain improvements to old houses, like putting in a bathroom or insulating the roof. Ask your local council what grants are available in your area for these purposes.

Leisure use

We began this chapter by looking at the different uses that are made of the local environment. One such use is for recreation and leisure. Many buildings we see around us have been designed specifically for leisure use, and many areas are set aside for this purpose. For example most towns have public parks or gardens. Other areas, although this was not their purpose, can be used for leisure activities. The Green belt around our towns is there to stop towns sprawling into the countryside, but it also provides a local area for walking, riding and relaxing.

Sometimes large areas of the countryside are designated as *National*

Parks. They too provide ideal walking and touring countryside, but again are not mainly for this. National Parks are areas of natural beauty which it has been decided should be preserved – they are the conservation areas of the countryside.

How many of these 'purpose-built' leisure facilities are there in your town?

Public parks and gardens

Recreation grounds

Children's playgrounds

Golf courses and putting greens

Leisure centres

Swimming pools

Tennis courts

Anything else?

Sample multiple choice questions

1 The term 'semi-detached houses' refers to houses which stand
   a) in pairs
   b) separately
   c) in a continuous row
   d) joined by their garages

2 The *main* function of the Green belt is to
   a) keep cars out of the countryside

b) provide leisure space for townspeople.
c) keep up land prices
d) limit the growth of towns

3   A product has good aesthetic properties if it
a) can be handled easily
b) has a pleasing appearance as well as being functional
c) the designer has taken cost into account
d) works effectively under any conditions

4   The purpose of planning permission and building regulations is to
a) make sure houses are built to the architects plans
b) make sure houses keep their value
c) make sure houses fit into the environment
d) allow people to build their houses as they want them to look

5   To find out about your local area's development plans you should visit
a) the local library
b) the local council
c) the local post office
d) the local police station

6   Building societies raise their money by
a) selling houses
b) taking in people's savings
c) borrowing from the government
d) rates and taxes

7   A low ceiling could be made to look higher by
a) painting it dark blue
b) painting it white
c) painting the walls white
d) painting the walls in thin vertical lines

8   What is the minimum age at which a person may obtain a mortgage from a building society?
a) 16 years
b) 18 years
c) 21 years
d) 25 years

9   Before building a house, permission must be obtained from
a) the neighbours
b) the local council
c) the government
d) the local housing association

10 Which of the following will *not* affect the aesthetic qualities of a chair?

a) its colour scheme
b) its symmetry
c) its cost
d) its styling

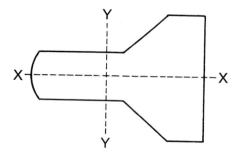

11 The shape shown here:
a) is symmetrical about XX only
b) is symmetrical about YY only
c) is symmetrical about XX and YY
d) does not have an axis of symmetry

12 Which of the following organizations does *not* lend money to house buyers?
a) building society
b) local council
c) housing association
d) bank

13 The purpose of 'zoning' in town planning is to
a) create conservation areas
b) restrict building development
c) group buildings into suitable areas
d) build new towns

14 The minimum size for a bedroom in a new house is fixed by
a) outline planning controls
b) building control regulations
c) zoning
d) aesthetic considerations

15 What proportion of people in Britain own their own house?
a) under 10%
b) 10–25%
c) 25–50%
d) over 50%

6

Power, pollution, and conservation

Power and energy

We have seen that many machines need power, or energy, to work them, because they are too big or too heavy to be worked by human muscles alone. Indeed, *energy* is one of the four things a factory needs to run its processes (along with *labour, capital* and *enterprise* — see Chapter 2).

Before the Industrial Revolution machines were relatively light and simple, and their power came from harnessing *animals*, the *wind,* or *water*.

Even at the start of the Industrial Revolution, the early factories used water-wheels to power their first machines. However as machines got heavier, larger and faster, and as they started to be made from iron, new and stronger power sources were required. During the 19th century *steam* was used as the major driving force of our machines, and it was produced by boiling water with our plentiful supplies of *coal*.

Electricity

During the 20th century electricity gradually replaced steam as the driving force of many machines. Electricity is more efficient than steam (less is wasted inside the machine), and is much easier to carry around the factory (by using wires). It also produces less pollution, and it was the building of the London Underground that really introduced electric power to Britain. Another common driving force in many factories is *compressed air*, which although it needs pipes to carry it around the factory is very powerful.

Compressed air, electricity and steam are all forms of energy, but they are not power *sources*, because they all need to be manufactured, or produced, from something else. Steam is produced by boiling water, using anything which will burn, like coal or gas. Electricity is produced in a generator.

The generator

A generator is a large cylinder with an axle going through it, containing coils of wire and magnets. Precisely how it works is not important here, although you may learn about it in science, but when the axle is turned quickly, electricity is produced. So something is needed to turn the axle. The dynamo or alternator in a car is a small generator, and the axle in that is turned by the fan belt connected to the engine.

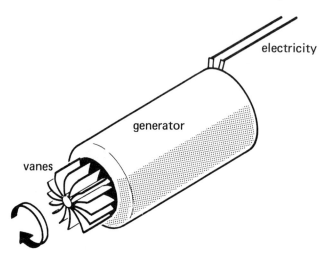

In a power station the generators are much bigger, and have vanes fitted to the end of the axle, forming a *turbine*. This turbine is turned either by *steam*, or by fast flowing *water*.

Electricity produced from water is called *hydro-electricity*. A dam is built at the top of a hill, and water travels from the dam down the hill in pipes to the turbine at the bottom. By the time the water reaches the turbine it is moving fast enough to turn the generator and produce electricity. It is only in mountainous areas that hydro-electric generation is possible, and Britain produces very little of her electricity in this way.

Steam generation

The vast majority of our electricity is generated by using steam to turn the turbines. Heat is needed to boil water to produce the steam, and this heat comes from three main sources – coal, oil, and nuclear fuel.

Coal is a *fossil fuel*. This means it was once alive, in the form of plants, but over millions of years has been compressed into the form in which we now use it. Britain has a great deal of coal, and is one of the world's major producers. So it is natural that most of our power stations use coal to make their steam. Coal mining is a primary industry.

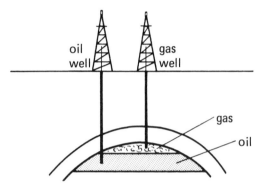

Oil, too, is a fossil fuel. It was once tiny sea creatures which, after millions of years of compression, have formed 'pools' of oil trapped under certain types of rock. Drilling through these rocks releases the oil. Natural gas is often found together with oil and was produced in the same way. Up until the early 1970s cheap imported oil was readily available and was used freely for burning by industry and power stations. The oil-producing countries then enormously increased their prices which threw much of the Western world into some financial chaos. One result was that it became worthwhile for Britain to start drilling for oil under the North Sea, and we now produce more than enough oil to satisfy our own needs from this source.

Nuclear fuel is based on *uranium* which is a *mineral*, not a fossil fuel (it was never alive). Uranium is mined in many parts of the world and only very small amounts of it are needed to produce huge quantities of heat. Once it has been processed the uranium is turned into either the very radioactive and unstable uranium '235', or into plutonium. The processing is very complex indeed and is beyond the reach of most countries. When more than a certain 'critical' amount of uranium 235 or plutonium is put together it reacts of its own accord, producing heat. If left uncontrolled it will explode (this happens in an atomic bomb). In a nuclear reactor the reaction is controlled to get the heat without the explosion, once again to turn water into steam to drive the turbines.

Nuclear reactors can be built small enough to power submarines, and because they use so little fuel and do not require air for burning, nuclear-powered submarines can remain underwater for very long periods. The Royal Navy has several such submarines.

Britain leads the world in nuclear technology and produces more electricity in nuclear reactors than any other country − 10% of our total power output. The original promises of abundant cheap electricity have not been fulfilled, however, because the technology involved has proved much more complicated and costly than expected. Theoretically, nuclear power could supply all our energy needs. A nuclear reactor uses so little fuel that the world's known deposits of uranium would last many centuries. However the substances involved are so dangerous that many people think our developments in this field should be halted.

Robbing the earth

Coal, oil and gas were made in the earth millions of years ago. The amount of them is fixed, and when it has gone there will be no more. And yet our industries and power stations are using them up at a colossal rate in their demand for heat and electricity. It is impossible to tell how long it will be before they run out, because we do not know whether, for example, other countries which are not industrial at the moment will start industries and therefore need their own energy. Even if world demand for energy only increases as it has done over the last twenty years, we will run out of fossil fuels in the years shown below:

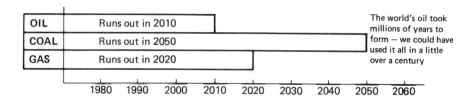

OIL	Runs out in 2010
COAL	Runs out in 2050
GAS	Runs out in 2020

1980 1990 2000 2010 2020 2030 2040 2050 2060

The world's oil took millions of years to form — we could have used it all in a little over a century

So the lights go out in 2050?

Most unlikely. As these fuels get scarcer and scarcer, so they will become more expensive. This will mean people will use less, and will look hard for new sources (like finding oil in the North Sea). So the figures given above are certainly too pessimistic. And the search will be on (many people say we should be doing more of this already) to find *alternative* sources of power. Many things will burn, but only oil can easily provide plastics and petrol. So it seems a bit crazy to waste this precious and scarce fuel in burning.

Alternative sources of power

The fossil fuels are called *finite* sources of power because they will run out (fairly soon). Let us look at some *renewable* sources of power which can never run out.

Solar power

We can use the sun's rays to heat water into steam. Experiments are going on with various mirrors and lenses to do this. Or we can save electricity by using solar panels to heat our water at home. Or we can get electricity directly from sunlight by using the special panels satellites have to power them in space.

Problems? What happens at night, or on a cloudy day? And it requires a panel one metre square to produce enough power to light a single light bulb on a sunny day!

The wind and the waves

Water is already used to produce electricity in hydro-electric power stations. And wind can drive generators directly. But whereas the generator stops when the wind drops, the *tides* never stop, and ways are being looked at of making the tides turn the generators.

Geothermal energy

In several parts of the world underground water is boiled by the heat in the earth's crust. Where this occurs it can be used to produce electricity, and does so notably in Italy and New Zealand.

The trouble with renewable energy sources is that they are either unreliable (like the wind), cannot be stored (like sunlight), or are likely to be prohibitively expensive (like wave power). Nuclear fuel, although technically a finite power source, is one answer if the dangers and technological difficulties can be overcome. And in the long run we will probably find out how to gather some of the energy from the sun which is now lost in space.

Questions

1   What were the *main* sources of power before the Industrial Revolution?

2   During the Industrial Revolution steam became a common form of energy. Which fuel was used to produce the steam?

3   What is a *finite* power source? List three.

4   What is a *renewable* power source? List three.

5   Why do we need to look for new sources of power?

6   The production of electricity is an example of *manufacturing industry*; electricity is made in factories called power stations. Which raw materials are used, and what processes are involved in its manufacture?

7   What are the advantages and disadvantages of the use of nuclear fuel to produce electricity?

Pollution

'A breath of fresh air'
The use of *finite* sources of energy to produce power causes waste products. Burning oil and coal gives rise to smoke; the use of nuclear fuels leads to the production of radioactive waste. The use of *renewable* energy sources does not produce waste however. Solar power, hydro-electric power, geothermal power, wind power and wave power are all 'clean' energy sources – there are no messy waste products. But we have seen that there are very great advantages in finite energy sources which will mean we will continue to use them, probably until they run out.

When is waste harmful?

If you throw an apple core into a field, or onto a grass verge, it may look messy, but it is not going to do any harm. Very soon the apple will be

eaten by an animal or bird, or will rot away. The sort of rubbish which disappears quickly of its own accord is called *biodegradable*. Just about all food is biodegradable, as is paper, material and wood shavings. That does not mean we should litter the countryside with it, because it spoils the look of our surroundings, but it is not a serious problem.

Much more serious is waste which is not biodegradable, because this will never disappear of its own accord, or will not disappear for a very long time. Tin cans, plastic bags, glass and china are not biodegradable. Bits of pottery can be found dating back thousands of years, which have never, and will never rot away. We have to be much more careful what we do with this non-biodegradable rubbish.

More serious still, though, is waste which is not only non-biodegradable, but positively harmful. The smoke from oil fires kills vegetation with its poisons, and destroys brick and stonework with its acids. The waste liquids from many industrial processes will kill the fish in our rivers and seas. Even the washing-up liquid we use is harmful to our waterways.

This harmful waste is what we called *pollution*, and is one of the most serious problems the world has to face.

Air pollution

The air we breathe is our life. It provides us with the oxygen we need to stay alive. Animals breathe in oxygen and breathe out carbon dioxide, and the earth's oxygen would eventually all be used up if there was no way of replacing it. It is replaced, however, by plants, particularly the enormous forests around the earth's equatorial belt. At the moment we are using more and more oxygen as we burn more and more fuel: and yet at the same time we are cutting down many square miles of forest each year to turn into paper. An area of the Brazilian rain forests the size of Wales disappears each year.

At the same time in our cities we are polluting the air with the exhaust fumes of millions of cars, burning up oxygen with the petrol and replacing it with carbon monoxide. In Tokyo they have provided oxygen masks on street corners to give extra oxygen for people who work in the streets all the time.

The motor car is actually the single most important cause of air pollution in Britain. As well as carbon monoxide, exhaust fumes contain sulphur dioxide (about which more later) and lead. The lead in petrol has reached such levels in the blood of children around major motorway junctions (like the Gravelly Hill interchange north of Birmingham – known as 'spaghetti junction' because of its twisting mass of roads) that there are fears it may cause permanent damage to their brains.

The smoke from coal fires used to cause serious pollution. When it

112

became mixed with the water particles in fog, the air turned to 'smog' – an almost unbreathable mixture which gave many people bronchitis and in some cases led to their deaths. This is one pollution problem we have solved. The Clean Air Act of 1956 made it compulsory for people in cities to burn smokeless fuel in their fires, instead of ordinary coal. The result is that there has been no smog since.

It would be possible to do the same with cars. There is already legislation controlling the gases cars are allowed to emit through their exhausts, which is why carburettors are now sealed and cannot be adjusted. This legislation could be made much more severe, as it is in California, but the cost would be a loss in power, and therefore a worse petrol consumption. And this is the central problem with pollution control – it costs money. Petrol can be made without lead in it, and it now has to be in the USA, but such petrol is more expensive than ordinary petrol.

One of our worst air pollutants is sulphur dioxide. This comes out of car exhausts, from factory chimneys, and from power stations. In the air it turns to acid, and it kills plants and damages stonework when it comes down to earth. The traditional way of controlling sulphur dioxide pollution was to make the chimneys taller. This was thought to work. The sulphur dioxide was taken into the upper atmosphere and disappeared. However it seems now that it does not disappear at all; it merely comes down to earth somewhere else.

British sulphur dioxide is being blown over the North Sea and is landing in Norway and killing the Norwegian forests. Thousands of lakes in Sweden can no longer support life, largely because of sulphur dioxide blown in from West Germany.

Half of our sulphur dioxide is produced by the Central Electricity Generating Board in their production of electricity. Perhaps this is another reason to look for alternative methods of electricity generation.

Water pollution

We use over thirty gallons of water a day each, for drinking, washing, washing clothes, and flushing the lavatory. And industry uses another thirty gallons a day for each one of us. And yet 'use' is probably the wrong word. Water is never used up, it goes round and round, evaporating from the seas and lakes, falling as rain, collecting in reservoirs, being washed in or drunk, going down the drain or the lavatory, back to the river and hence to the sea again. If we are short of water, we really mean most of it is in the wrong place for the time being – in the seas or clouds instead of our reservoirs.

The oxygen in water keeps fish and water creatures alive in just the same way as the oxygen in air keeps us alive. And just as we are removing the oxygen from our air, so too are we removing it from the water, so that the fish cannot live. There are two ways of polluting water – 'killing' the water by removing the oxygen from it, and poisoning it by adding harmful chemicals.

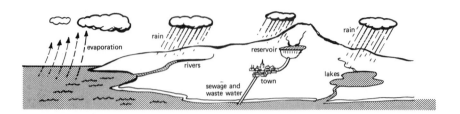

Killing water

Human sewage is not harmful in itself — ask any gardener who puts horse manure on rhubarb or roses. However our population is much too large for our sewage to be allowed to fertilize the ground and it has to be treated and poured into the rivers and sea. This treated sewage removes oxygen from the water. The River Thames has only just become fit for fish to live in again, after a long period as a 'dead' river.

Many industrial wastes, and detergents, also remove oxygen from the water. They too, like with the Thames, could be treated differently, but again it is expensive.

Poisoning the water

Other industrial wastes, particularly chemicals, poison the water, again resulting in the death of the fish. These chemicals — mercury is one of the worst — are difficult or impossible to remove and remain in the water, eventually finding their way to the sea. A great many industrial processes use chemicals, and it is only comparatively recently that controls on their discharge have been brought in. Chemicals, called *pesticides*, used to kill insects on crops, are also brought down to the rivers by the rain. Pollution of the sea is a particularly spectacular form of pollution, because it can affect hundreds of miles of coastline. If an oil tanker breaks up, hundreds of thousands of tons of oil can be discharged onto the surface of the sea, from where it will be taken by the tide to the nearest coastline. So the oil will pollute both the sea and the beaches.

In fact oil, though spectacular, is not as serious a problem as chemicals, because it is eventually biodegradable.

A few worrying facts

*The River Trent carries into the sea each year:
 350,000 tonnes of chlorides
 850 tons of zinc

114

400 tons of nickel
300 tons of copper
*Minimata, Japan 1953 − 46 people died after eating shellfish poisoned with mercury waste
*Spain 1970 − A whole industry based on oysters was wiped out when a ship loaded with dieldrin − a pesticide − ran aground
*The British Navy has altogether dumped over 175,000 tonnes of poison gas canisters in the North Sea and the Atlantic

Land pollution

You will all know locally of areas of land which could be used for growing crops, or for houses, but which have been laid waste instead. Huge slag heaps, waste tips, and quarries spoiling the countryside. The National Coal Board alone produces 10 million tonnes of waste every year, much of it piled up in huge heaps. Perhaps you have seen derelict cars lying around, or broken down buildings.

Most of this is not harmful. Slag heaps can be flattened, or used for road building. Holes can be filled in. Unproductive areas can be covered with fresh soil. Nothing will grow on slag heaps because they are really minced-up rock. Plants need the nutrients in rich topsoil. But poor soil can be turned into topsoil by treating it with sewage sludge, lime and nitrogen: it is merely a matter of cost.

However, some waste is dangerous. Old chemicals dumped in drums can seep out and spread poisons, sometimes explosive poisons, round about them. Often no one knows what has been dumped on tips in the past, or if they do know, they do not know how to make them safe. Whole tips have exploded sometimes for unknown reasons concerned with unsafe industrial waste.

The law and pollution

Both water and land pollution is now covered by legislation, since the passing of the Control of Pollution Act in 1974. No one is allowed to dispose of waste into rivers, lakes or the sea, or to dump it in holes in the ground, without first obtaining permission from either the Water Board, or the local authority's Environmental Health Department. Some firms have now set themselves up as specialists in dealing with dangerous waste, and can often make safe waste products from industry.

Nuclear waste

Nuclear waste is a particular problem, because it is particularly dangerous, and long lasting. A speck of plutonium would kill you if it got on your skin. If you were buried with the plutonium still in place, and someone dug you up in a thousand years' time, then the plutonium would kill them too. And yet we have whole tanks of waste from our nuclear power stations, and do not quite know what to do with it. One thing is for sure − it can't stay in the tanks. It will be perhaps half a million years before it is safe, and we cannot guess at what might happen to the tanks in this length of time. Various suggestions are being made like burying it in holes deep in our mountains, or sealing it in glass and dumping it at sea, but the right answer has yet to be found.

What can you do about it?

You may think there is nothing *you* can do about the problems of pollution, but this is not true. It is because of pressure from ordinary people, sometimes working in groups like Friends of the Earth, that we have done as much as we have in Britain to control our pollution. And we are well ahead of the rest of the world in many areas of pollution control. (One exception being in car pollution where we lag well behind the USA.) First of all you can set a good example; don't drop litter − particularly non-biodegradable litter. Buy goods in as little packaging as possible (so there is less to throw away). When you see examples of pollution, complain − to your MP or local councillor. And finally, walk or use a bicycle where possible, thereby not adding to the pollution caused by motor vehicles.

Suggested work

1 What is meant by pollution?

2 What is biodegradable rubbish?

3 List the *main* causes of air pollution, and say what laws have been passed in an effort to prevent them.

4 Why is chemical waste discharged into water such a problem?

5 What is a pesticide? In what way can pesticides cause pollution?

6 Do you think that the dangers of nuclear waste are a sufficient reason for slowing down our development of nuclear power? What reasons can you give for your answer?

7 Which Local Authority department is responsible for the control of pollution?

Further things to do

1 Are there any derelict sites near you? Why are they derelict? What could be done with them?

2 What problems do your local firms have in disposing of their dangerous waste? How do they solve them?

3 You might like to get someone from Friends of the Earth to speak to you about pollution, and what you can do to help prevent it.

Conservation

Look back at the table earlier in this chapter showing when our fossil fuels are likely to run out. Coal will run out in 2050; oil in 2010; and gas in 2020. We saw then that one possible answer to this problem is to use less of these fuels, by cutting down waste. This using less of something to make it last longer is called *conservation*.

Conservation of power sources

We can make our power sources last longer by using less coal, oil, gas and electricity. And since these fuels are expensive, we will also save money at the same time. One obvious way to save them is to cut down on what we waste. If you leave a light on when you are not in a room, you are wasting electricity. If you leave a car engine running unnecessarily, you are wasting petrol. And if you have your house heated when there is no one at home, you are wasting whatever fuel provides your heat. We can all save considerably if we are sure that we only use fuel when it is necessary.

When we heat our house, we do not also want to heat the road outside as well. And yet a lot of the heat does go to waste doing just that. To stop this waste we rely on *insulation*. We insulate our house so that less of the heat passes out of the house and is therefore wasted.

Heat disappears from a house which is not insulated in the following order:

Most goes through the roof
Next largest amount goes through the walls
Then through the doors
Then the windows

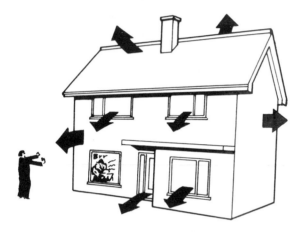

So the first thing to insulate is the roof. All new houses have to have insulation above the upstairs ceiling in the loft. This is *loft insulation* and often takes the form of thick fibreglass matting, or heaps of tiny polystyrene balls. Owners of old houses without loft insulation can apply for a grant to help them do the work.

The walls of a house are often built in the form of two layers of brick, or breezeblock, with a gap, or cavity, between them. Filling the cavity with special substances can cut down the heat loss through the walls. This is *cavity wall insulation*, and although it is expensive, it can soon pay for itself it terms of the fuel it saves.

Heat escaping through the doors usually goes under or around them. You may be able to feel the draught. Cutting out these draughts by fitting *draught excluders* is a relatively cheap way of saving fuel. And keeping doors closed will obviously help keep the heat in the room where it is wanted.

Glass is quite a good insulator on its own, but it can be improved a lot by heavy curtains. If these are drawn as soon as it gets dark, they will help keep the heat inside as the evening gets colder. Another way of improving the insulation of windows is by *double glazing*. This involves fitting a second pane of glass over the window on top of the first, or completely replacing the window with a double-glazed unit. Double glazing has extra advantages in that it cuts down noise from outside, and condensation, but it is a very expensive way of getting a comparatively small fuel saving. The previous three improvements are much better value.

Another improvement, where central heating is concerned, is to make sure that a working *thermostat* is fitted. The thermostat will turn the heating off when the required temperature is reached, and not bring it on again until the temperature has fallen. And with central heating, make sure all the radiators in rooms you are not wanting heated are turned off, and that radiators on outside walls have a sheet of aluminium foil stuck on the wall behind the radiator. (This little improvement, which costs virtually nothing, and is invisible from the room concerned, can save up to 3% of your fuel bill on its own.)

Firms, too, are working to conserve fuel. They use the same principles of *care* (with lights and doors), *controls* (like thermostats), and *insulation*.

Conserving other materials

It is not only finite sources of energy which require conservation. Many of the raw materials we use are also running out at an increasing rate. Here is another table showing the dates when various materials commonly used by industry will no longer exist in their natural state.

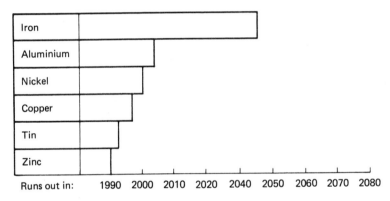

	Runs out in: 1990 2000 2010 2020 2040 2050 2060 2070 2080
Iron	
Aluminium	
Nickel	
Copper	
Tin	
Zinc	

As with the table of fossil fuels we looked at earlier in the chapter, these dates are almost certainly very pessimistic. They assume that the increasing rate at which the world is using these materials will continue. This is probably not the case; as they get rarer they will get more expensive, and will be used less.

It is difficult to think of alternatives though. Perhaps the most serious case is that of iron. Our whole industry is founded on iron and steel (which is made from iron). Trains, boats and planes; cars, machines and cranes – all are made from iron and steel. Cars can be made of fibreglass or plastic, but this comes from oil, which is scheduled to run out in 2010; boats and ships can be made from wood, as they used to be in the past, but they would be heavier (because the wood has to be much thicker than

119

the iron) and smaller (because the wood is weaker and needs more supporting). In any case we do not have an ever increasing supply of wood. It was a shortage of wood in Britain which led to the need for coal (in part) in the first place, and remember the statistic about an area of trees the size of Wales disappearing from the Brazilian forests each year.

And yet there is really no need for iron to run out in 2045 if we change our ways of using it, and *conserve* the iron we already have. The two main ways of conserving iron, copper, wood, and other raw materials are by *cutting down waste*, and by *re-cycling*. Re-cycling means using the material a second time after its first use has finished, instead of throwing it away.

Cutting down waste

Many goods we buy are deliberately designed to have a short life, after which they will be thrown away. How many times have you thrown out an article of clothing, or a pair of shoes, not because they are worn out, but because fashions have changed and you no longer like them? Sometimes fashions are changed deliberately by manufacturers so that this will happen. The practice is known as *planned obsolescence*. A car's body shape might change slightly to encourage people to buy the 'new model'; firms might advertise an 'improved' type of television to try and persuade people their old models are out of date.

You can beat planned obsolescence by either refusing to be taken in by these advertisements, or by buying things which are perhaps slightly more expensive, but which are 'built to last'.

It is easy to see why some firms go in for these practices. There is the old story of the man who invented an everlasting light bulb who was offered a great deal of money by a bulb manufacturer to hide his product away – the manufacturer was worried that if everyone bought the new everlasting bulbs they would never need to change them again and he would go out of business. And the firm which makes steel beer barrels now has to look for breweries abroad to buy their products since most of the British breweries have now bought them, and since they last forever, will not need to buy replacements.

These are not good arguments. If people do not need to buy new lightbulbs, or shoes, or cars, or beer barrels, they will spend their money on something else instead. The firm may need to change to making something else, but they will still be in business, the consumers will be better off, and our iron will last much longer.

We could persuade firms to do this by putting a higher tax on goods which only had a short life, thereby making them more expensive and unattractive. This would not be necessary if people chose of their own accord only to buy long lasting goods though.

Disposable items

Some goods are made to be used once, then thrown away, like disposable knickers, razor blades, plastic forks and spoons, newspapers. These are very wasteful of our natural resources. In other cases although the product itself will last, it is packed in a whole mass of paper, cardboard, plastic and polystyrene, all of which is immediately thrown away. Sometimes a certain amount of wrapping is essential for protection, hygiene, or to contain a loose product, but it is often well overdone.

Non-returnable bottles   It used to be the practice that glass bottles were always returned to be refilled, and in some cases, like milk bottles, this is still the case. Much more often though bottles are simply thrown away. This idea of non-returnable bottles was brought in by Schweppes, and the Friends of the Earth recently returned a huge quantity of these bottles to Schweppes to make the point that their idea is rather wasteful. At least glass is made from raw materials of which we have plenty − more worrying is the move to disposable plastic bottles, which are made from our dwindling supplies of oil.

What can we do about it?

Don't buy disposable articles unless you really have to. If you do buy them, ask yourself whether they can be re-used. Plenty of people wash up plastic knives and use them again for their next picnic; the bags your vegetables come in can often be used for other purposes if they are kept; don't buy goods in excessive packaging − why pay for the box (which, make no mistake, you do) when what you want is the thing inside it? And do you know of anyone who can make good use of old newspapers?

Re-cycling resources

Many things we throw away can be turned to good use again, by separating out from the waste what is still valuable, and only finally getting rid of what is completely used up. For example, when a car is scrapped, it still contains a large quantity of iron which is still perfectly good iron, just as good as the day the car was made. This iron can be collected from the scrap yard, melted down, and used again. This is re-cycling. Cars are large, and comparatively easy to recycle, but a large proportion of our rubbish is not large, and is all mixed up together with other bits and pieces. Consequently the bits of iron, the other metals, the paper, the glass, and the food which we throw away is simply either dumped or burnt, because this is easier than going to the trouble of sorting it out. And all the things mentioned there can be re-cycled. Even old food can be re-cycled to form compost for fertilizing soil. And much of the real rubbish which is left can be burnt to provide heat or power.

We are getting much better at re-cycling rubbish. Several local authorities now operate re-cycling plants, and in some cases these can pay most or all of the cost of emptying the dustbins in the first place. It is obviously

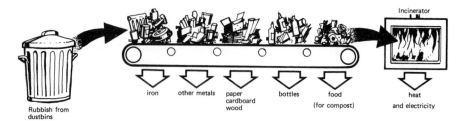

iron | other metals | paper cardboard wood | bottles | food (for compost) | heat and electricity

Rubbish from dustbins

Incinerator

better not to have to throw something away, than it is to throw it away and re-cycle it, however.

Suggested work

1 What does *conservation* mean?

2 What is the purpose of insulation?

3 If you are thinking of insulating your house, what is the *first* place you would look to check the present insulation? Why?

4 The management of Thomas Harris Limited, a small factory, have asked their workforce to suggest ways the company could save fuel. What would you suggest they do, in terms of improving the care of their staff, their heating controls, and their heat loss?

5 When will the last steel motor car be made, if we continue to increase our use of iron at the present rate?

6 Why is wood not a suitable alternative to iron?

7 What examples can you give of planned obsolescence? How can ordinary people help beat this practice and so conserve resources?

8 Make a list of the things you throw away which could be recycled. Does your local authority have a re-cycling plant? If not, why not? (Ask them.)

9 Think of some of the things you or your friends have bought recently. Consider the goods' packaging. Was it all necessary for safety, hygiene and protection? Or was some of it simply wasteful?

Looking for new supplies

As well as re-cycling, we are always on the look out for new supplies, or alternative materials. Right now it is difficult to think of any alternatives for iron, but it may well not be in the future. A hundred years ago very few people would have dreamed that we would discover substitutes for wood, metal, wool, cotton, fertilizer or glass, and yet we now have substitutes for all these in the form of plastics and chemicals derived from oil. It is a pity that oil will run out so soon, and even more of a pity that we per-

122

sist in burning such a valuable material!

We continue to find oil in new places, however, and this process of new discovery will go on, not only for oil, but for our other resources as well.

There are large quantities of metals and other minerals hidden under the deserts and seas of the world, and under the ice mountains of Antarctica. As the price of our raw materials rises, so it will become worth looking in these difficult and expensive mining areas. We are increasing our own timber resources by planting new forests over large areas of the countryside. Away from the earth there are metals and minerals in abundance. A human being first walked on the moon in 1969 — we cannot guess when the first moon mine will be opened, but we can be sure that it will happen in time. And perhaps in 500 years time space freighters really will travel from outer space bringing valuable cargoes of iron ore, aluminium, tin and zinc. It is perhaps a pity that the one thing they will almost certainly not bring is oil, since oil, a fossil fuel, can only have formed on a life-bearing planet, and we only know of one of those, and we have almost used up all its oil already.

The problem gets worse

We are making great strides towards solving the problems of pollution and conservation, but we must remember that these problems have only just begun. Only a small part of the world is industrialized at the moment. The USA and Britain between them use half the world's total supply of electricity, serving only one twentieth of the world's population. Imagine what will happen to our natural resources when the rest of the world catches up to our level of usage. On the face of it the world will then use ten times as much oil, coal, iron, timber and nuclear fuel as at present each year. And that is assuming our own use of these resources stays constant. In fact our own consumption of electricity has doubled in the last ten years.

And increasing industrialization is only one factor making the problem worse. The size of the world population is growing at an alarming rate too, and as the rest of the world industrializes, this population growth might increase even more.

Britain's population remained more or less steady up to the beginning of the Industrial Revolution. The increasing wealth, the improvements in medicine, and the better methods of food production which started to appear over the next hundred years led quickly to the quadrupling and quadrupling again of the population. This has now begun to happen over the rest of the world.

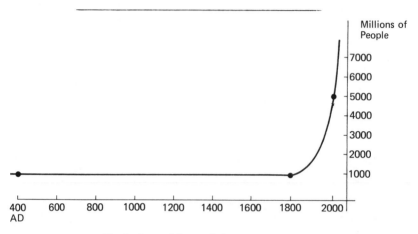

Rise in the world's population

This dramatic increase in the world's population is referred to as the *Population Explosion*.

Feeding the world

As better medicine increases the populations of the developing countries, we read of drought and famines leading to millions of deaths. Does this mean that eventually there will be just too many people to feed? In fact it doesn't. There is a limit to what better medicine can do, and it is really increased food production and better diets which in the long run will keep the population rising. So increased food production will go hand in hand with the technological advances and growth in population throughout the world.

The world's production of food is not fixed, it can and will increase enormously as the population grows. And eventually the population will stop growing, just as it has in Western Europe and the USA. Already great steps are being taken by governments and the United Nations to persuade, or in some cases force, people to have fewer children, by marrying later or using methods of birth control. In China couples have been forbidden to marry before the age of 30, and then not allowed more than two children, and in India men have been offered money or gifts if they will be sterilized.

Things to do

1 Why do you think that as a country becomes 'developed' its people choose to have fewer children, or none at all. Note that in Britain people do not have to be persuaded to be sterilised; they will pay for it!

2 Why will the world not run out of food as the population continues to grow?

3 Why will the world run out of other resources like iron, oil and timber at an increasing rate as the population in developing countries grows?

Sample multiple choice questions

1 Which of the following is *not* a fossil fuel?
   a) coal
   b) oil
   c) uranium
   d) gas

2 Which of the following ways of generating electricity produces least pollution?
   a) nuclear power
   b) oil-fired generators
   c) coal-fired generators
   d) hydro-electricity

3 Which of the following uses of oil could easily be substituted for?
   a) generation of electricity
   b) propulsion of cars
   c) production of plastics
   d) production of fertilisers and drugs

4 Conservation of resources might best be achieved by
   a) keeping their price steady
   b) changing from renewable to finite fuels
   c) persuading individuals to cut down on waste
   d) increasing planned obsolescence

5 What is the major source of air pollution in Britain?
   a) the motor car
   b) the Central Electricity Generating Board
   c) heavy industry
   d) the oil industry

6 Which of the following types of water pollution is the most serious?
   a) the release of sewage
   b) the discharge of chemicals
   c) accidents to oil tankers

d) the dumping of old cargoes

7   Which of the following energy sources is *unlikely* to be used up in the foreseeable future?
a) oil
b) nuclear fuel
c) coal
d) gas

8   The main purpose of planting new forests over large areas of Britain is to
a) improve the looks of the countryside
b) increase our oxygen supply
c) provide leisure facilities
d) increase our supplies of timber

9   The reason behind insulating a cavity wall is to
a) reduce condensation
b) reduce noise
c) reduce heat loss
d) reduce humidity

10   Which of the following is a major air pollutant?
a) sulphur dioxide
b) carbon dioxide
c) nitrogen
d) hydrogen

11   The advantage of nuclear power generation of electricity is that it
a) is completely safe
b) produces no waste
c) relies on plentiful supplies of fuel
d) produces plutonium as a by product

12   Using the iron in scrap cars to produce new cars is most accurately described as
a) conservation
b) pollution
c) generation
d) recycling

13   A finite resource is one which
a) will last for ever
b) can be recycled
c) will sooner or later be used up
d) is present in outer space

14   A serious pollutant from motor car exhausts is
a) dieldrin
b) lead

c) mercury
d) copper

15 The effect of the Clean Air Act 1956 was
a) the establishment of National Parks
b) the establishment of smokeless zones
c) the removal of cars from certain city centres
d) the removal of sulphur dioxide from the air

7

The individual in society

'No man is an island'

We all live together in one, rather crowded, group of islands. We depend on each other in many different ways, and we come into contact with people we know and people we do not know almost every day. We are a *society* of people all living, working and playing together. If we did live alone on a desert island, we could do absolutely as we pleased all the time. But since we live in a society, what we do has to be affected by the people around us.

Unlike many people in the world, we live in a *free* society. This means that we are 'free' to do just about anything we want, providing what we do does not interfere with other people's freedom. How far our freedom goes is determined by our traditions, or customs, and by our laws. These customs and laws give us certain *responsibilities*, and certain *rights*. Our responsibilities make us protect other people's freedoms, and our rights make other people protect our freedoms. One person's responsibility is another person's right.

Our responsibilities

We have a general responsibility to help other people, particularly those too old, too young, too sick, or too weak to help themselves. We also have a responsibility to help society run smoothly — to protect our own and other people's safety and property, and to help the police. When we help an old lady across the road, or give up our seat on a bus to a pregnant woman, or dive into the river to rescue a struggling child, we are fulfilling these general responsibilities.

These responsibilities are customs, rather than responsibilities by law. You are unlikely to be prosecuted and fined if you do not give up your seat to an elderly person with a walking stick, but other people may not think very highly of you. Other responsibilities are enforceable by law though, and you can be punished, or made to pay compensation, if you do not fulfill them.

Responsibility to respect property

You are not allowed to go onto another person's land or into their house without permission. Even a police officer needs a Search Warrant to enter a house unless he or she has reason to believe a crime is being committed there, or is in 'hot pursuit' of a lawbreaker.

Responsibility to protect reputations

You are not allowed to say or write anything which would damage a person's reputation, unless it is true. You cannot, for example, say that George Roberts is a lousy plumber, or Thomas Smith is a thief, unless you could prove, in a court of law if necessary, that these statements were true. Saying untrue damaging things is called *slander*, and writing them is called *libel*.

Responsibility to treat people of other races fairly

There has never been any distinction in law between people of different races or colour; it is intended that they should be treated equally. But since the Race Relations Act was passed in 1965 it has become an *offence* to discriminate against people on the grounds of their race or colour. This applies to the staff of public places and most employers. It is also an offence to stir up hatred against people of another race or colour.

Responsibility to serve the country

Everyone has a responsibility to help their country when called upon to do so. Thus the government can *conscript* people into the armed forces in times of war. In fact, Britain is one of the few countries which does not practise conscription as a matter of course, war or no war. One is not allowed to pass information on to a potential enemy, or, if a member of the Civil Service, to divulge government secrets. This prohibition, governed by the Official Secrets Acts, is thought by many to be too extensive.

Similarly, when called upon, adults have to serve on a jury, or give evidence as a witness in court, or help the police if reasonably able to do so.

Since Britain is a free country, we are allowed to do anything which is not specifically forbidden by law, so the whole idea of *rights* is a bit misleading. Our rights are the opposite of our responsibilities — the right not to have our home entered, the right not to be slandered or libelled, the right to be treated fairly, the right to have witnesses and a jury at a trial, and so on.

Put another way, we can say what we like, providing it does not slander anyone or stir up racial hatred. We are free to join any religion we wish, or to marry someone of any race. We are free to travel and live where we choose, providing we respect other people's property. We can leave the country if we want to. To people living in Poland, or East Germany, or Argentina, or the USSR, or Chile, or South Africa, or many, many other countries, these rights would seem quite extraordinary.

Protecting our rights

Our rights are very valuable, and envied all over the world. It is up to each one of us to protect them by making sure we fulfill our responsibilities. Remember that someone else's right is our responsibility, whether that be the right to walk the streets at night without being molested, or the right to a fair trial with a jury.

However since not everyone does fulfill their responsibilities, we need the police force to ensure that the law is enforced, and our rights protected.

The law

The police do not make the laws — they only enforce them. Laws are made by the Government and the Houses of Parliament. And it is another of our basic rights to vote in elections, or to stand for Parliament ourselves.

There are two main branches of the law, Criminal and Civil. *Criminal law* is concerned with the things we are forbidden to do, and is enforced by the police. *Civil law* is concerned with arguments between individuals, or individuals and firms, where one is claiming compensation from the other for doing something wrong. The police do not usually deal with civil law.

The first job of the police is to stop people breaking the law — the prevention of crime. The second job is, if the law has been broken, to find out who did it and take them to Court. The Court will decide if the person accused is guilty or innocent, and if guilty, will punish them.

The way the police do these jobs is carefully controlled, and we have a number of rights to protect us against possible unfair treatment. Let us look at how the police work by taking a hypothetical (made up) case.

A woman walking home from Bingo is attacked, and her handbag stolen. The attacker was a young man. She starts screaming and is seen by a policeman who goes to her assistance. He radios for a patrol car which scouts round the district, and meanwhile takes a statement from the woman, and a description of her attacker.

The patrol car comes across a young man in a street half a mile away, and the driver stops to question the young man. He is not satisfied by the man's reasons for being in the street, and asks him to come to the police station.

What are the young man's rights? The policeman cannot force him to go to the police station against his will, but any person is required by law to help the police if reasonably able to do so. To fail to assist when asked amounts to obstructing the police in the course of their duties.

In fact he does agree to go with the policeman. The woman has meantime said that her attacker had long black hair, and on learning this the police driver realises he has got the wrong man, his suspect being blond. He apologises and lets the man out of the car, thanking him for his help. As he leaves, the man mentions that he saw another youth running up a nearby alley, possibly carrying a handbag. The policeman continues his search and finds this second youth. He asks him to accompany him to the station, and this time the youth refuses. However the policeman now has good grounds for believing he may be the right person, and so *arrests* him.

Now what are his rights? It is a basic right that no one can be held prisoner against their will, that is they cannot be stopped from walking away if they wish. However, if a person is reasonably suspected of having committed an *arrestable* offence, then a police officer (or anyone else, for that matter) can *arrest* the person, take them to the police station, and question them. They do not have to say anything. An *arrestable* offence is an offence that carries a penalty of five years' imprisonment, or more,

130

which includes all serious offences such as theft and crimes of violence.

In fact he denies having anything to do with the crime. So the police arrange an Identity Parade. They have this youth standing in a line with several other similar youths, and ask the woman who was attacked to walk down the line and see if she can pick out her attacker. She picks the youth the police arrested. She also identifies a bunch of keys found in the youth's pocket as being from her handbag. The police then are satisfied the youth is the attacker, and *charge him* with the offence.

The police cannot decide if a person is innocent or guilty, or punish them. That is up to the courts. And it was established over 700 years ago, in the Magna Carta, that no one could be held in prison without a trial. So, having arrested someone, the police must charge them and take them before a court as soon as possible, usually within 24 hours. If they fail to do so, anyone can apply to a judge for a writ of *Habeas Corpus*, and secure the person's release.

The police decide that the youth in our story will be taken to court the next day, and so they lock him in a cell for the remainder of the night. They could have let him go, and then called him to court some time in the future, had they wanted to. The next morning he appears before the local *magistrate*.

The Magistrates Court

Anyone arrested must appear as soon as possible in a magistrates' court. There is no jury, but a panel of two or more magistrates (or occasionally one). They will *try* (decide whether innocent or guilty) and *punish* anyone convicted of a summary, or minor offence. They can also try and punish more serious offences, such as theft, if the accused person does not object, providing they do not think the circumstances are too serious. Very serious offences they will not try, but will hold a *preliminary enquiry* to decide if there is enough evidence against the accused person to justify sending them to a Crown Court for trial. There is a limit to the sentences a magistrates' court can give, but they are allowed to send a guilty person to the Crown Court for *punishment*, even if they have tried the case themselves, under certain circumstances.

Most people who appear in court plead guilty, but our youth is not one of these. He denies the charge. The magistrates listen to the police evidence and decide that it is sufficient to justify a trial. It is a very serious offence, theft with violence, or robbery, and will be tried at the Crown Court. The magistrates will *remand* the accused youth, either in custody, when he remains locked up until his trial, or *on bail*, when he is released, but may have to promise a sum of money should he fail to appear for his trial.

Right to bail Bail can only be refused if the accused is likely to commit further offences, to interfere with witnesses, or has already failed to appear when called.

Our youth is bailed.

When the date of his trial arrives, he is sent a summons to appear in court. If he did not appear, a warrant for his arrest would be issued, and he would be arrested and held in custody until a new court hearing could be arranged. In fact he does appear. He has seen a solicitor, who has arranged for a barrister, to represent him in court. The police also have a barrister representing them, as the prosecution. The jury is selected from those members of the public called for jury service, and will comprise twelve people. The court is presided over by a judge. Both the prosecution, and the youth's defence, then present their cases. The evidence against the youth is that he was picked out in the Identity Parade, and had the woman's keys on him. His defence is that he found the keys, and that the woman was mistaken. After hearing the evidence and the defence, and listening to any witnesses called (like the woman herself, and the first man the police stopped), the judge will send the jury away to reach a verdict. At least ten of the twelve jurors must agree on a verdict, and they can take as long as they like. They must decide whether, beyond all reasonable doubt, the accused person is guilty.

In this case, they decide he is guilty. It is now up to the judge to decide on a punishment. First, he asks the police if the youth has been convicted of any previous offences. He finds he has — he attacked a woman the previous month, and an old man the year before. Taking this into account, the judge sentences the youth to Borstal Training.

Types of punishment

Death by hanging (Capital Punishment) In the year 1800 some 150 crimes were punishable by death (including theft), but this list was whittled down by stages until by 1971 only treason and piracy were capital offences. (Murder ceased to be punishable by death in 1965). It is most unlikely that anyone will be hanged in Britain nowadays, even for these crimes. The last man to be hanged for treason was William Joyce, in 1946.

Prison Before 1800 people were usually only sent to prison to await trial; being in prison was not a punishment in itself. However, with the drop in the number of capital crimes, and the decrease in places to *transport* prisoners to, away from Britain, prison became a punishment in its own right. Nowadays, most crimes carry a *maximum* prison sentence which is only likely to be used in really exceptional cases (theft is ten years, robbery is life imprisonment). Murder is an exception — the sentence is always life imprisonment, sometimes with a *minimum* recommendation from the judge (eg 'at least 25 years').

If a prisoner is given a sentence of a specific number of years, they are granted *remission* of one third of the sentence after serving two thirds the number of years, if they have been of good behaviour while in prison.

That is, a person sentenced to six years will be released after four unless they have broken prison rules. In addition a prisoner may apply to be released *on licence* after serving one third of their sentence, or the minimum period of a life sentence. Such an application will be considered by the *Parole Board* and, if granted, will have conditions attached. A person who breaks parole conditions may be recalled to prison.

A prison sentence of less than two years may be *suspended* for up to two years. This means the guilty person does not actually go to prison if they keep out of trouble for the period of suspension.

Fine   A fine is a very common sentence and can be imposed for any offence, sometimes in addition to something else. Fines can vary according to a person's means, and can be backed up by a prison sentence if they are not paid. A magistrates' court can order a guilty person to pay up to £2000 compensation (or more in the Crown Court) in addition to any fine or prison sentence, the compensation, unlike the fine, going to the victim of the crime.

Community service order   Where an offender is ordered to serve from 40 to 240 hours helping in the community. It is in place of a prison sentence, and if the order is not carried out, the offender may be recalled and sent to prison.

Probation   The idea of probation is to help the offender lead a better life. He or she will have to see a Probation Officer regularly, and may be told where to live or work. If the offender does not stick to the terms of the Probation order, he or she can be recalled to court fined up to £400 for the breach, and given a different sentence.

Discharge   If the offence was very minor, and the offender was of previous good character, the court may grant a conditional, or absolute discharge. A conditional discharge means that the person can still be punished if he or she gets into trouble again, but an absolute discharge ends the matter. This is very different from *case dismissed*, which means the judge decided there was not enough evidence, and the accused is therefore innocent.

And for young people:

Instead of the above, the court can order the young person to go to

An attendance centre   Up to twelve hours, spread over several weeks, of instruction and supervision.

A detention centre   Up to six months away from home for a 'short, sharp shock!'

Borstal training   From 6 months to 2 years detained at a Borstal which is like a young person's prison. Only a Crown Court can order Borstal Training.

Legal aid

You will also have noted that our attacker above had to engage a solicitor and a barrister. This is very expensive, but a person on a low income can ask for *legal aid* to pay some or all of the costs. Solicitors showing the legal aid symbol will give help and advice under the legal aid scheme.

Scotland

Scotland has its own legal system, which works a little differently from the English system we have described. The main difference is that the police do not prosecute themselves. They send the papers of the case to the Procurator Fiscal, and he decides whether a prosecution should be made, and if so, prosecutes the case himself. There are also some differences in procedure and the make up of the courts.

Suggested work

1 What does it mean to say 'No man is an island'?

2 What are the general responsibilities of a person in our society?

3 What is meant by slander and libel?

4 About our imaginary case:
   a) What is 'Habeas Corpus'?
   b) What is the difference between a magistrates' court and a Crown Court?
   c) If the attacker had not had any previous convictions, do you think he would have been given the same sentence? What else might have happened to him?
   d) How many people serve on a jury?

5 Try and arrange a visit to a court to see for yourself how it operates. You could also ask a local police officer to speak to you about the procedures followed when arresting or questioning people.

6 What sentences would you consider appropriate for the following crimes?
   housebreaking, speeding, vandalism, manslaughter (killing someone by accident), drunk and disorderly.

Protection of our rights as consumers

When we buy goods and services from other people, we have a right to expect certain things from them. Look at these situations:

> SITUATION 1: I bought a pair of wellingtons yesterday, and they leak. What can I do about it?

> SITUATION 2: This dress I bought last week won't fit. The shop refuses to change it. What can I do?

> SITUATION 3: The hairdresser cut my hair too short. Do I have to pay him?

> SITUATION 4: I paid £50 deposit for a holiday and now I don't want to go. Can I get my money back?

> SITUATION 5: I ordered a glass-fronted book-case, and now it has arrived I've been told I have to pay extra for the glass. Can they do this?

We are now talking about *civil law*, which controls agreements and arguments between individuals. What would civil law say about the situations above? First, a word about contracts.

Contracts

Our dealings as consumers are all bound up around contracts. A contract is a legal agreement between two people where both promise to do something for the other. A contract is enforceable by a court if one of the parties does not keep to their side of the agreement. If you agree to pay a shop £50 for a suit, then you have a contract – you must pay the £50; they must provide the suit. Note that a contract cannot be one-sided. If you promise to give a friend £25, that is not legally binding unless he or she has promised to do something for you in return.

Age of majority

You become an adult in the legal sense at 18 in Britain. That is the age you can vote, marry (you can marry at 16, but only with your parents' consent, unless you live in Scotland when it's 16 anyway – that's why people used to elope to Gretna Green), buy a house, get a passport, make a will, and *enter into contracts*. Since you cannot enter into most contracts until the age of 18, you may find your parents have to sign things on your behalf. About the only things you can't do at 18 are stand for Parliament or sit on a jury (both 21).

The law and contracts

In general, what it says in the contract goes. However most things we buy are not subject to full written contracts, and many of the terms of the contract are taken for granted. So there are a number of laws to control contracts. These laws even take precedence over written contracts − that is a shop cannot hold you to an agreement you sign taking away your rights under these laws.

The Sale of Goods Act 1979

This Act says that everything a shop sells you must be of *merchantable quality*. That is to say the goods must be fit for the intended purpose and free of major defects. In other words, they must work properly. If you buy the goods from a shop, then it is the shop, not the manufacturer, who is responsible. This applies even if the goods were packed into a sealed container in the factory and bought by you from the shop in the same sealed container. It is still the shop with whom you have your contract.

In Situation 1 above, the wellingtons were not fit for the intended purpose because they leaked. Therefore the shop did not fulfill its contract and you can demand your money back − not a credit note, unless you agree, but your money back.

Usually the purpose is obvious − wellingtons for walking through puddles, a lawn mower for cutting grass, a pen for writing with − but sometimes not so. Should a jacket keep out the rain? Should a carpet stand up to having water sloshed all over it? In cases like these, it is up to you to satisfy yourself that they are suitable. If the shop says so, then they must be. If you ask for a waterproof jacket, then it must keep out the rain.

Note that if you discover a fault after buying something and the shop offers to repair it, you then lose your right (if you agree to the repair) to have your money back.

Guarantees

A guarantee, or warranty, is an offer made by the manufacturer to repair or replace faulty goods. This is in addition to your rights under the Sale of Goods Act, and it is up to you whether you take advantage of it. If goods are faulty when you buy them, it is usually better to ask the shop for your money back and refuse a repair. If they go wrong later, it might be difficult proving they were at fault when you bought them, so it would then be wise to take the repair offer from the guarantee. The reason manufacturers offer guarantees is to give customers confidence in their products and a remedy if they go wrong.

What to do about it

First, go back to the shop. Nine times out of ten they will give you your money back, a replacement item, or a credit note which you will be happy to take. If they don't, write to their manager or Head Office (they must tell you where it is — just asking them might be enough to change their minds) as quickly as possible — like this (keep a copy);

Dear Sir,

Last Monday, 23rd June, I bought a portable television set from your Birmingham Corporation Street branch. I specially asked for one which would work in my bedroom. Since taking it home I have been unable to get any picture at all in my bedroom, and only a very poor one in my living room. Since the television is not suitable for the purpose intended, that of watching television in my bedroom, I reject it under the Sale of Goods Act and claim back the purchase price of £87.50. I also claim from you £2.50 to cover my bus fares visiting the shop last Wednesday to return the set, which they refused to accept.

Yours faithfully,

Joe Milligan

If you don't get an answer, or they try and fob you off (unlikely if they are a big, reputable company) you will have to see a solicitor for your next step — go to the Citizens Advice Bureau.

When you would be in the wrong

You cannot demand your money back just because you don't like the goods, or they don't fit, or you've changed your mind. Some shops, like Marks and Spencer will let you do this, but they don't have to. Similarly, once you've paid a deposit you have a contract and must see it through. And if goods are sold as 'sub-standard' or 'seconds' the Act does not apply.

Trade Descriptions Act 1968

It is illegal (and a criminal offence, as well as a civil wrong) to make a false or misleading description of goods a trader is offering for sale.
Examples: '100% cotton' 'One owner' 'Only 2 years old' 'Reduced to half-price' '250 yards from the beach' 'Will last a hundred years' 'Used by royalty'

All the above descriptions must be true. If they are not, the trader can be prosecuted, and you could claim your money back if you had bought something on the strength of the description.

Exceptions

A lot of things are not covered by the Act. Descriptions of houses, expressions of opinion ('the best in the world'), obviously untrue claims ('your friends are sure to like it'), and descriptions of books and films are not covered. Neither are goods sold by people who are not traders (ie private individuals). Also a trader can tell you that a description is maybe not true, and thereby avoid the Act — like this:

Sale goods have not necessarily been offered for sale in this branch at the higher price	This mileage is not known to be correct

Descriptions do not necessarily have to be untrue; if they are misleading an offence has been committed. A trader could not defend 'used by Royalty' on the grounds that a man called Mr Royalty had used his goods.

What to do about it

Go to your Trading Standards Officer (under your local authority in the 'phone book). If he or she agrees with you proceedings can be taken and get you compensation. (In Scotland this would be done by the Procurator Fiscal). It doesn't make any difference whether the trader knew the description was false or not — he or she has still committed an offence.

Unfair Contract Terms act 1977

Some irresponsible firms rely on the 'small print' in a contract to escape from their obligations.

'The firm is not responsible in any way for any loss or damage which may occur to films sent for processing, however caused'.

Before the passing of the Unfair Contract Terms Act, this clause would have prevented someone claiming the value of their films from the company even if the firm had carelessly left them in the developer too long, or had lost them, or left them on a bus, or . . . . .

Such clauses, exclusion clauses they are called, are now invalid, or meaningless, unless the firm concerned can show that they are fair and reasonable.

Case history: Mr Hodgson took his car through an automatic car wash. The brushes whirred round, but there was no water. When his car emerged, the paintwork was scratched. He complained to the garage, who pointed out a notice at the entrance of the car wash saying that the gargae would not be responsible for any damage caused by their car wash machine. Mr Hodgson took them to court, and the court held that the clause was not reasonable and fair, and so the garage had to pay compensation.

What to do about it

See a solicitor, through the Citizens Advice Bureau.

Sociology Dept.
Univ of London
Goldsmiths' College
New Cross, SE14 6NW

Other protections

Unsolicited Goods and Services Act 1971
If you are sent through the post goods *that you did not order*, you can either write to the firm telling them to come and collect their goods, and if they don't, keep them; or do nothing, in which case the goods become yours after six months. Whatever you do don't pay for them!

Weights and Measures Act 1979
This makes it illegal to sell certain goods at short weight. If you buy a gallon of petrol, the pump must actually give you a gallon. This would be covered by your contract with the shop or garage, but it is difficult or impossible for the customer to check. The local authority has inspectors who call unannounced at shops, pubs and garages to check the accuracy of scales, drink measures and petrol pumps. The Act also covers various things like the percentage of actual meat in a sausage, and the proportion of real orange juice in orange drinks. (Orange *juice* must be all real juice from oranges; orange *squash* must be at least 25% orange juice, and orange crush or orange drink needn't have any real orange in it at all).

139

Mail order protection scheme

MAIL ORDER PROTECTION SCHEME

Advertisements in this newspaper are required to conform to the British Code of Advertising Practice. In respect of mail order advertisements where money is sought in advance of the despatch of goods the Code requires the advertiser to despatch goods within 28 days, unless a longer period is stated. Where goods are returned to an advertiser, undamaged, within 7 days, the purchaser's money must be refunded, plus the cost of returning the goods. The reader should retain evidence of despatch.

If you order goods from mail order advertisements in this newspaper and pay in advance of delivery you will be considered for compensation under the Scheme if the advertiser becomes insolvent or ceases to trade provided that:

(a) you have not received the goods, or a refund in respect of returning same, **AND;**

(b) you write to the Advertisement Manager of this newspaper, stating the facts, not earlier than 28 days from the date of the order and **NOT LATER THAN THREE MONTHS** from the date on which the advertisement appeared.

THE SCHEME ONLY COVERS ADVANCE PAYMENT SENT IN DIRECT RESPONSE TO AN ADVERTISEMENT IN THIS NEWS-PAPER. IT DOES NOT COVER: –

(a) Classified advertising;

(b) payment made in response to catalogues, brochures, etc. received as a result of responding to such advertisements;

(c) advertisers offering services as opposed to goods;

(d) gardening advertising except for durable goods;

(e) claims where payment is made with Access or Barclaycard and where the cost of the goods is over £100. In this case claims should be made to the Credit Card Company concerned.

Full details of the Scheme are available by sending a stamped and addressed envelope to Mail Order Protection Scheme, Newspaper Publishers Association Limited, 16 Tooks's Court, London EC4A 1LB.

Questions

1 Look back at the *five* situations we started with. Can you give the people their answers now?

2 List the *five* main Consumer Protection Acts we have covered in this section, and say briefly what protection each one gives.

3 I promise to give my car to my next door neighbour. The next day I

change my mind. Can he make me give it to him? Why not?

4   What does a Trading Standards Officer do?

5   You have bought a pair of slippers. When you went to get the washing in while wearing them you trod in a puddle and the sole fell off. Have you a claim under the Sale of Goods Act? Would it make any difference if you had told the shop that you were in the habit of doing this and they said the slippers would stand up to it?

6   You have bought an electric drill in a sealed box. When you take it out you find it will not work. You go back to the shop and they tell you it is nothing to do with them, and suggest you write to the manufacturer. You know your rights, though. Draft a letter to the manager of the shop demanding your money back. What would you do if he ignores your letter?

7   Look around for examples of exclusion clauses you think are unfair and for notices avoiding the Trade Descriptions Act. Try dry cleaners, garages, and large shops with sales on.

Keeping your body healthy

It has been said that our body is like a machine, and that just as a machine needs fuel to keep it running, so our body needs food. This is not a good comparison. An engine needs only one type of fuel to power it, with perhaps some oil to lubricate the working parts as well. Our bodies are much more complicated than this. They require many different types of food for a lot of different purposes. Although we may eat as much as we like, and may even be rather fat, if we do not eat the right types of food, we will not be healthy in one way or another.

We need food to stay alive, but we also need food to:

Keep us warm (80% of what we eat goes to maintaining our body temperature).

Help us grow, or in adults help to replace old and damaged body tissues.

Give us energy.

Keep our bones and teeth healthy.

Protect our eyes.

The amount and types of food we eat is called our *diet*. The importance of different types of food in our diet has been known for many years, and was first discovered by a British doctor, James Lind in the eighteenth century. Many sailors prior to this discovery had died from *scurvy* during their long sea voyages. Lind found that by including fruit like oranges, lemons and limes in their diet, scurvy could be prevented. This is how British sailors came to be known as 'Limeys'.

Many people even nowadays do not have a good diet. We have high rates of heart disease, tooth decay and obesity (being overweight), which are caused in part be our eating the wrong foods. Let us look at the reasons why we need different types of food.

Foods for growth and energy

Foods which provide for the growth and replacement of body tissues are called *proteins*. Proteins also give us energy.
These are the protein foods:

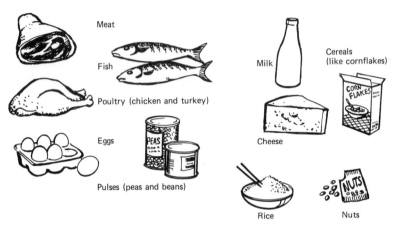

Not all these foods provide the same type of protein, and too much of some of them can be harmful (see later), so it is important to eat a *variety*. We should ideally have three servings of protein every day.

Example: Breakfast − Cornflakes or an egg
            Lunch − Baked beans or cheese
            Dinner or tea − Meat or fish

Foods for energy

Foods which give us energy are called *carbohydrates*. We could get all the energy we need from proteins, but this would be rather expensive. Also we need *fibre* in our diet which is present in many carbohydrate foods, but not in most proteins.
These are carbohydrate foods which contain fibre:

bread (particularly wholemeal bread)   spaghetti
potatoes   noodles
rice   anything else made from flour
cereals

Note that rice and cereals also contain protein. We should ideally have three servings of these fibre foods every day. In the above example of breakfast, lunch and dinner, if we added a piece of toast to the breakfast and the lunch, and had potatoes with the meat or fish, the diet would contain enough carbohydrate.

142

Food containing minerals

Two minerals are essential for a healthy body — calcium and iron. Without calcium our teeth and bones will be affected, as will our blood without iron. About the only food containing calcium is milk, and foods made from milk like yoghourt and cheese, so these are essential in any diet.

Young people who are still growing should have the equivalent of a pint of milk every day, and adults half a pint. One small yoghourt or 50g of cheese is equivalent to half a pint of milk. Remember that milk is just as good if it is taken in tea or coffee, but you would need to drink at least ten cups of coffee to take half a pint of milk.

Iron is present in a lot of foods — liver, egg yolk, kidney, and green vegetables. Vegetables are the best source though, because they also contain certain other trace elements which are necessary to us in very small quantities.

Now our breakfast could be: Cornflakes with milk, toast and a cup of tea
Lunch: Beans on toast and a yoghourt
Dinner: Fish or meat, potatoes and peas or green beans

On another day breakfast could include an egg, and lunch or tea might be liver, with a drink of milk.

Vitamins

Vitamins were only discovered fairly recently, and yet are essential in small amounts to prevent disease, and to protect the eyes and skin. They are grouped together into four types, Vitamins A, B, C and D.

Vitamin B is found in most foods, and so is almost bound to be present in a good diet. Vitamin D is produced by the body from sunlight without the need for food, but for people who do not go out of doors very much is also found in milk and eggs. Children living in dark, grimy cities used to suffer from ricketts, which is a disease caused by lack of Vitamin D.

Vitamin A is found in milk products, and also in fruit and vegetables.

Vitamin C is the vitamin which prevents scurvy, amongst other things. It also keeps the gums healthy and helps our body to heal cuts and wounds. Vitamin C is found in fruit and vegetables, particularly in fruit. Providing we eat fruit and vegetables every day and an orange from time to time, we will get all the vitamins we need. Fruit is important in preventing constipation.

Fruit *juice* (not squash — see the Weights and Measures Act earlier on in this chapter) is equivalent to eating a piece of fruit.

Summary

A healthy, well-balanced diet, should contain all the following *every day*:

Three servings of protein foods
Three servings of carbohydrate foods
At least two servings of vegetables
At least one, preferably two or even three pieces of fruit, or fruit juice
Half a pint of milk (a pint for young people who are still growing), or the equivalent in yoghourt and cheese.

These are not really minimum requirements, they are just what you need – no more and no less. And remember it is important to vary the types of food each day to pick up the trace elements.

Foods we don't need which can be harmful

There are three types of food which used to be thought important, but which it is now believed we do not need at all. They contribute to obesity, and many doctors blame them for the rise in heart disease. They can make food taste nicer, or make it more interesting, but they should only be used in small amounts, and should be avoided where possible. They are:

Fats: Butter, margarine, lard and cooking oil. Where possible, foods should be grilled instead of fried. Chips contain a large amount of fat (from their cooking) and should not be eaten all the time in preference to other forms of potatoes. Cakes contain a lot of fat, as does cream. The average British diet contains large amounts of fat, which is one reason we have such problems from obesity and heart disease. There is some evidence that *polyunsaturated* fats are better for us than other fats, and so you should ideally use polyunsaturated margarine on your bread or toast rather than butter or ordinary margarine.

Sugar: Sugar contains no nutrients at all except refined carbohydrate and is completely unnecessary. It too contributes to obesity and heart disease and is responsible for much tooth decay. It should only be used when essential for taste, or the occasional sweet. (Sweets are virtually 100% sugar.) Many people prefer tea and coffee without sugar when they get used to it. We eat on average 45 kg of sugar a year, 250 times more than we did 100 years ago.

Salt: Unlike sugar, small amounts of salt are necessary in our diet, but these small amounts are all accounted for naturally in a balanced diet, or in the salt added during cooking. Too much salt is now considered a cause of high blood pressure and heart disease.

If you stick to these rules
You will be strong and healthy.
You will not be overweight.
You will have smooth skin and nice hair.
You will have a greater protection against disease and heart trouble.

Suggested work

1 'Drinka Pinta Milka Day!' Why?

2 'An apple a day keeps the doctor away', but an orange would be even better. Why?

3 Make a list of the different types of food we need each day. Say what each one does for us, and the types of foods it is contained in.

4 Look at your own diet. Write down everything you ate yesterday, and compare it with our suggested summary of foods. How does it compare? Which foods are you not eating that you should be? Which foods are you eating which you should not be?

5 A friend of yours is constantly troubled by tooth decay and constipation. What would you suggest he or she included in their daily diet to combat these things?

6 Suggest your own well-balanced daily diet of foods you like which meets the requirements of our summary.

More protection against disease — immunisation

A good, well-balanced diet will make us more resistant to almost all diseases. But it won't stop us becoming ill altogether, particularly in childhood. In the past, perhaps half of all the children who were born died fairly quickly from one disease or another. Nowadays children are *immunised* against the old killer diseases to give them an *immunity*, or make them safe against the disease. If children stopped being immunised, the diseases would not come back quite as badly as before, because of better diets, but they would certainly return, and would certainly still be fatal in many cases.

The best example of immunisation is against smallpox. A worldwide programme of vaccination has now wiped this disease off the face of the earth.

Why immunise children?

Two reasons: to protect the individual child, and to cut the disease down in the community, so that children who have not been immunised because they are too young or have some special *contra-indication* (a medical reason why they can't be immunised) won't catch it either.

Against what

This table shows the main diseases against which immunisation is used, and the possible dangers of the disease without immunisation. You can sometimes catch a disease even if you have been immunised, but it will not be a very serious attack.

Disease	What would happen if you caught it	Age when you are immunised, and how
Diphtheria	Severe throat infection, usually leading to death	These three diseases are immunised in one injection called the Triple Vaccine at 3 to 6 months old, then again at 8 to 11 months, and again two months later.
Tetanus	Caught after a bad cut; high risk of death	
Whooping cough	Can lead to lung damage, brain damage, and death	
Polio	Can cause paralysis of one or more limbs, or the whole body	Immunised by drops in the mouth at the same three times as the Triple Vaccine
Measles	In rare cases can cause brain damage	Injection at about 15 months
Tuberculosis	Affects the lungs	At about 12 or 13 (the BCG)
German measles (Rubella)	Not very much, but the disease can damage the unborn baby in a pregnant woman.	Girls only, at 11 to 13

Boosters are given for diphtheria, polio and tetanus at age 5 (whooping cough is no longer dangerous at 5), and for polio and tetanus at about 16 to 18 (when diphtheria is no longer dangerous).

It is up to each family to make sure their children are protected by their local doctor or Health Centre. Parents do not have to have their children immunised, and some parents chose not to have the Whooping cough vaccine (but still had the other vital bits of the Triple Vaccine) after a report suggesting the immunisation might have itself caused brain damage. The result now is that there is far more Whooping Cough around than would otherwise be the case. Children are far more likely to be damaged by catching the disease than by having the injection, unless they have some contra-indication, which would be explained by the doctor, and would result in a fever after the first of the Triple Vaccines, and in which case no further injections would be given.

A couple of questions

1 Which diseases have you been immunised against? (You may need to ask your parents.)

2 Can you design a poster of leaflet persuading parents to have their children immunised? The Health Education Council's leaflet begins: 'Just a few moments' discomfort for years of protection'.

What to do with your money

Why, spend it of course! Yes, but not all of it. Once you start working, you will have to learn to make the money you get each week or month stretch to pay for as many of the things you want as possible. This process is called *budgeting*, and your budget will be a list of your expected income, and your planned expenditure.

The trick, and difficulty, is to keep your expenditure low enough to be below your income, so you have a bit left over. Some things you have no choice about — you have to spend money on them, and these would come first in your budget: housing and food.

These might well come together if you are living at home, or staying in digs. How much will you give your parents to keep you? How much will your landlord or landlady charge?

If you live on your own, or share a flat with others, you will also have to pay a share of the electricity, gas and telephone (if you have one) bills. These will vary enormously, but you can find out from your parents roughly what they might be. Then you will have to pay for your travel to and from work, and your lunches at work. How much might this be?

You will be helped in managing your money if you have a bank account, or post office account, or building society account to put your money in when you get paid. (You may have to have an account because your pay might go straight into it — see next chapter.) There are a number of different types of account:

Current account at a bank: With this type of account you get a *cheque book* which allows you to pay money to other people without using cash, just by writing a cheque. If the bank gives you a *cheque card*, your cheques are guaranteed up to an amount of £50, and so will be accepted by anyone. Note that it is a criminal offence to write a cheque if you do not have the money to pay for it in your account, unless you have made an arrangement with the bank.

Deposit, savings, or building society account: With these accounts you do not get a cheque book, but your money is safe, and the organization pays you some *interest* on the money you have in the account. The interest a building society pays is generally higher, if you pay tax, than

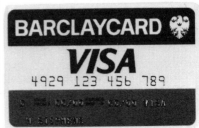

that a bank pays, so a building society is perhaps the best bet, particularly for savings.

There is a great deal to be said for not spending all your money, but saving a bit each week. You will want to buy clothes, or save for a holiday, or buy other things that you will not be able to afford out of your budget. Even £1 a week builds up to £55 after a year (with interest), and £5 a week would give you £275 after a year. It is best to put your savings into a different account from your usual money, so you are not tempted to spend them too easily!

Sometimes though, you will want to buy something expensive immediately, rather than wait the very long time it might take to save up for it. Examples could be a motorbike or car, a stereo system or television. In this event you will have to borrow the money to pay for it. You will have to pay *interest* on the amount you borrow, and must remember that the repayments will go on for many months or years. Are you sure your budget will allow for these repayments?

Where to borrow from

1   Your parents. Always try them first. They may have money they are not using, which they would be happy to lend you, often without charging any interest at all.

2   Your bank. This is next cheapest. It is always better to borrow from a bank than buy something on hire-purchase, even though the bank may charge you something like 18% interest.

3   Hire-purchase. Only do this if you have already asked your parents and a bank. The cost is often well over 30%.

4   Trading cheques. With these you are given a cheque by the Trading Cheque Company to buy the goods, which you gradually pay back. It is very expensive (maybe 85% interest) and if you have to resort to this perhaps you should consider not bothering.

Other methods

You could buy from a catalogue (see Chapter 2) or by using a Credit Card, like Access, Barclaycard or Trustcard. With a credit card you do not need a cheque or cash, you simply sign for the goods and are sent a bill at the end of the month for all your purchases. You have a *credit limit* telling you the maximum you can spend with your credit card, and providing you keep below this you can pay off all or only some of your bill each month, holding the rest over to a future month. More expensive than a bank loan, but usually cheaper than H.P.

A PROJECT FOR YOU − Knowing how much you might earn, try and draw up a budget for yourself. Do you have a bank or building society account already?

Sample multiple choice questions

1 Which of the following snacks contains the best balance of types of food?
   a) orange juice and a yoghourt
   b) an apple and a Mars bar
   c) a piece of cake and a slice of toast
   d) a glass of orange squash and a bag of crisps

2 If an accused person is granted legal aid, this means
   a) they need not go to court
   b) they will not be sent to prison if they keep out of trouble
   c) they will get free legal help
   d) they are allowed to have a barrister representing them

3 The age of majority is
   a) 16
   b) 17
   c) 18
   d) 21

4 Which of the following Acts of Parliament deals with Consumer Protection?
   a) Health and Safety at Work Act 1979
   b) Race Relations Act 1976
   c) Equal Pay Act 1970
   d) Sale of Goods Act 1979

5 To which of the following places would a person go wishing help in getting their money back for faulty goods?
   a) Citizens Advice Bureau
   b) Weights and Measures Office
   c) Health and Safety Executive
   d) Health Centre

6 The credit limit applied to a credit card holder tells him/her
   a) the most he can spend on one item
   b) the least he must pay back each month
   c) the maximum amount he can borrow
   d) that he has reached his maximum limit

7 If you bought a drill in a sealed box, and it turned out to be faulty, who would be responsible for giving you your money back?
   a) no one, unless there was a guarantee
   b) the shop you bought it from
   c) the manufacturer
   d) the wholesaler

8 The purpose of calcium in a diet is to aid
   a) growth
   b) energy

c) teeth and bones
d) blood

9 Habeas corpus is connected with
a) whether we have to go to the police station when arrested
b) how long we can be held by the police before going to court
c) who represents us in court
d) whether we can be sent to prison for three months or more

10 A cheque guarantee card guarantees payments of
a) all cheques
b) all cheques up to a value of £30
c) all cheques up to a value of £50
d) all cheques up to the holder's credit limit

11 If a garage tried to escape liability for damaging your car because of small print in the repair contract, you might be able to ignore the small print because of the
a) Unsolicited Goods and Services Act 1971
b) Trade Descriptions Act 1968
c) Sale of Goods Act 1979
d) Unfair Contract Terms Act 1977

12 Which of the following diseases is not normally protected against by immunisation?
a) german measles
b) whooping cough
c) epilepsy
d) polio

13 What does a Probation Officer do?
a) represents the police in court
b) supervises offenders instead of their going to prison
c) runs Attendance Centres
d) advises the police on arrest procedure

14 Which of the following accounts pays the most interest to a tax payer?
a) a bank current account
b) a bank deposit account
c) a building society account
d) a post office national savings account

15 Oranges are one of the best sources of
a) Vitamin D
b) Calcium
c) Iron
d) Vitamin C

8

The individual at work

At some times during your life you have little or no choice about what you do. Before the age of 5 you are totally dependent on what your parents do. From 5 to about 16, depending on exactly when your birthday is, you have to attend school. When you reach the school-leaving age, though, you have a choice about your future. Will you stay on at school; or go to College; or get a job, and if so, which one? Perhaps there are no jobs available, in which case you might take a place on a government training scheme. Many of you will already have taken at least a part of this decision about what to do.

Unless you choose not to work, or become unemployed, or become too sick to work, you may be affected by such decisions for the rest of your working life until you reach the retirement age (65 for men, 60 for women), and so the right choice is very important.

Young people did not always have such a choice. Before the Industrial Revolution most people (65% of the population) worked on the land. Those who did not generally did whatever their mothers or fathers had done, perhaps as domestic workers. While they were children they had learned the skills of the job by helping their parents, and would rarely consider anything else. There was very little choice.

Even during the last century there were relatively few jobs to choose from. Most people worked in Primary industries, like mining, or in manufacturing. Both these types of work were then very *labour intensive*, that is they required a large number of workers to keep them going. They are not so today. Increasing numbers of machines, and more advanced technology, have led to far fewer people being employed in factories. Instead, as we saw in an earlier chapter, they are employed in a wide range of service industries.

So wide is the range of jobs today that it would take over *eleven hours* to list them all! There are over 40 000 different jobs to choose from.

Sorting out jobs

Tinker, tailor, soldier, sailor, marine engineer, nuclear physicist, ...

We have already looked at ways of sorting out different types of firms, and this also sorts out the different jobs. But it is sometimes useful to look at jobs in terms of the type of skills involved, rather than what type of firm the job is concerned with. For instance if you asked someone 'What do you do?', they might answer 'I work for British Leyland.' That tells you something, but you could well still ask: 'But what do you *do* there?', and they might then say: 'I'm a typist', or: 'I'm a fitter', or whatever. Since there are 40 000 different things they might do, we need some way of classifying them, or sorting them into groups.

The registrar general's classification

For convenience, jobs are sorted into six different groups, according to the type of skills and training the jobs require. The main groups are groups I to V.

Group I – Professional and executive. These are the jobs at the top of industry, or the so-called *professions* of doctor, lawyer, teacher, and so on. People in these jobs will have University Degrees, and will have spent up to seven years training after leaving school at the age of 18. Other examples are chartered engineers, judges, air-line pilots, vets, and senior officers in the Armed Services.

Group II – Administrative. These are jobs which require high qualifications, but not usually degrees, where the people concerned are involved in running (or administrating) businesses, shops, factories, or government departments. Many in the civil service, the police and managers of shops or managers in firms are in this group.

Group III is the largest group, and is split into two:
Group IIIa – Clerical. People who work in offices, libraries and other organizations which employ staff to work with paper or words rather than machinery.

Group IIIb – Skilled manual. *Manual* work is work where the skill lies in a person's hands as well as his or her head. Manual workers frequently work with machines. *Skilled* work means that the job requires a long period of training, usually an apprenticeship of three or four years after leaving school. Once skilled, the worker becomes a *craftsman*. He or she may be described as 'time-served', which means successfully completing an apprenticeship, and will have papers to prove it. Examples of skilled work, or *trade*, are plumber, joiner, fitter, turner, motor mechanic, bricklayer, toolmaker, and so on.

Group IV – Semi-skilled. Semi-skilled work requires some training, but it takes a few weeks or months, rather than years, and does not usually involve any qualification. Machine operators are often semi-skilled.

Group V – Unskilled. This is work which anyone could learn in a matter of hours. The fact that it is easy to learn does not of course make it easy to do. It may be unpleasant, dangerous, and unpopular. Examples are road-sweeper, barman or woman, labourer, and refuse collector.

Group VI is really an extra group, which is a number of jobs which do not fit in anywhere else, like actor, pop-star, and footballer.

Social class

A person's *social class* is related to the job he or she does. Jobs in Groups I and II are usually described as 'middle-class', and those in III, IV and V as 'working-class', although many people in Group III are now doing the sorts of things middle-class people do, like owning their own homes, as they earn more money, and increasingly regard themselves as middle-class.

If a child gets a job in a different group from his father or mother, particularly if it puts him or her in a different social class, the child is said to be *socially mobile*. Mobile means 'moving', and social mobility is moving from one class to another. This used to be virtually impossible. Not so nowadays, though, when the job you do depends not on your parents, but on your own *interests, skills, and education*.

Suggested work

1   What is an apprenticeship?

2   What does it mean to be 'socially mobile'?

3   What does it mean if an industry is 'labour intensive'?

4   Write out a list of the *five* main occupational (or job) groups, from I to V, briefly describing each, and giving *five* examples of jobs in each one.

5   What do the following people do: fitter, turner, toolmaker?

6   Play 'Desert Island Jobs'. Imagine you are shipwrecked on a desert island. Which *three* people, according to their jobs, would you most like to have with you? Compare your answers with those of your friends.

7   Just as everyone in a football team or tug-of-war team plays their part, and the team would not be the same without any of them, so *all* jobs are necessary to our way of life, whether they are in Group I or Group V. Or are they? Can you think of a job which is not of some benefit to society?

We don't need no education . . .

Oh yes we do! Apart from anything else, the jobs we can apply for and get depend on the type of education and qualifications we have received. There are many different ways of getting training and qualifications — here are some of them:

Schools

The main way most people get their basic qualifications, up to CSE and 'O' level. Those wishing jobs requiring higher general qualifications may stay on to take 'A' levels.

Correspondence courses

A way of learning from home. You send off for lessons which arrive by post, and which you complete at home.

'On-the-job' training

If your employer wants you to learn more, or if you are doing an apprenticeship, he will train you while employing you. He might do this completely 'on-the-job' at your place of work. Or he might send you to a College one day every week for 'day-release'. Or he might send you to College for several months, even a year, at a time. This is called 'block-release', and is becoming more and more common, particularly with large firms.

Colleges of further education

An alternative to school for 'A' levels, and a way of taking 'O' levels for those who missed them at school. Attendance can be full-time or part-time, day or evening. Colleges are particularly suitable for skill training related to definite jobs, like hairdressing, catering, or clerical jobs, or general vocational training. Many students take City and Guilds, TEC or BEC qualifications in preference to 'O' and 'A' levels.

Sandwich courses

You spend some time at College, then go to work, then go back to College to finish your course. All the time you will be paid by your employer, or by an *Industrial Training Board*. These are special boards set up to oversee training in their own industry. If they consider that not enough training is being done by firms, then they will train people themselves, often through Sandwich Courses.

What qualifications will I need?

Very difficult to say, but as a guide look at this table:

Type of job	Type of qualification to start	Type of qualification you end up with
GROUP V — Labourer	None	None
GROUP IV — Operative	Some C.S.E.'s useful	None, but you will be trained and experienced
GROUP III — Craft, Trade or Clerical	C.S.E.'s, 'O' levels or C.&G. Foundation Certificate useful	Recognised (often all over the world) trade qualification, like C.&G.
GROUP II — Administrative	4 'O' levels	Technician qualification, O.N.C., or specialist certificate
GROUP I — Professional	'A' levels	Degree or H.N.D.

PLASTERERS ROUGHCASTERS ROOF TILERS

required by Miller Construction Northern for work in the Edinburgh area. Bonus payable.

Please telephone:

Mr Dodds

031-332 2585,

or

031-445 4858 after 6 p.m.

28759

WAREHOUSE PERSON

required by playground equipment suppliers situated on western outskirts of Edinburgh. Own transport required. Good salary and bonus.

Apply stating age and experience, to

**THE SECRETARY
GAME AND PLAYTIME LTD.
RODDINGLAW WORKS
RODDINGLAW
EDINBURGH EH12 9DB**

34862C

---

251 SHOP AND STORE STAFF

SCHOOL LEAVER

We wish to employ a Junior Salesman/Saleslady for our electrical showroom in Haymarket, Edinburgh. If you have a bright personality, smart appearance and good school results and would like to start a career in retailing, you might be the person we are looking for.

Initially, please write telling us about yourself to:

Mr W. McARTHUR,
TRIDENT,
56a DALRY ROAD,
HAYMARKET,
EDINBURGH.

64808Q

ROYAL COLLEGE OF PHYSICIANS OF EDINBURGH

ADMINISTRATIVE ASSISTANT

required to assist with a fund raising appeal; part-time (17½ hours per week). Appointment up to 2 years. Graduate with some similar experience preferred.

Salary in the region of £2,750 per annum.

Applications including particulars of previous experience and names of two referees should be sent by 26th July to: The Secretary, Royal College of Physicians of Edinburgh, 9 Queen Street, Edinburgh EH2 1JQ, from whom further particulars can be obtained.

08940W

ROBERT ANTHONY
INVESTMENT JEWELLERS

require smart young full-time assistant. Previous experience in selling and display an advantage. Varied work and good prospects. References essential.

Applications in writing to:

108b ROSE ST., EDINBURGH.

40475T

---

256 SITUATIONS GENERAL

12 JOBS AVAILABLE NOW

Due to continued expansion, we have immediate vacancies for 12 young people to join our success story. If you are 16-27, keen, ambitious, live within 10 miles of Edinburgh, are presentable and available now, then phone up today for early interview. But hurry, the first 12 successful applicants will be appointed. Make sure you're not unlucky 13.

031-666 0300
10 a.m.-4.30 p.m.
or
031-336 3810
5 to 7.30 p.m.

07787N

OFFICE SENIOR ASSISTANT
(30-50)

with good shorthand typing and clerical experience. Ability to work on own initiative. Salary negotiable. Pension.

Apply in writing giving full details to **The Clerk and Treasurer, Churches and Universities (Scotland) Widows and Orphans Fund, 137a George Street, Edinburgh, EH2 4JY.**

19532G

ESTIMATOR

Edinburgh-based company require an estimator for metalwork contracts, in particular structural steelwork, balustrading and railings, etc.

Reply to:
**BOX NO. A806
SCOTSMAN
PUBLICATIONS LTD.**

238241

---

256 SITUATIONS GENERAL

CAPITAL DECORATORS require experienced painters and decorators for all types of private, commercial and industrial painting. Only experienced applicants need apply. Contact Mr Mullen on 556 0020 between 5 p.m. and 7 p.m. any evening. 17164E

PEOPLE needed to train as counsellors to aid others in distress or with problems: this new technique results in a well and happy person: all welcome to apply. Contact Dianetics, 20 South Bridge, 556 5074/5: Fife counsellors wanted as above, 0592 744124. 11626E

PLANT OPERATOR, immediate long-term contract position for experienced Poclain P60 operator. Phone now on 031-226 5233. SOS Bureau (agency). 18527P

TAXI DRIVERS. Two drivers wanted, alternating day and night shift: rental system: cab 12 months old. Tel. evenings 669 5134. 48850W

WINDOW CLEANER, holiday relief, driving licence advantage: 337 5240. 56311V

---

257 BANDS/MUSICIANS/ARTISTS

HEAVY ROCK BAND seeks vocalist. Bob 339 5281. Dave 667 1675. 35934C

VOCALIST or guitar vocalist for modern club band. 665 7377 6-7.30 p.m. 17007D

You can often use the qualification you end up with in one group, as the starting qualification for the next. For instance a fully trained and qualified craftsman could go on to take a technician qualification without 4 'O' levels, using his trade qualification instead. That is if he wanted to, of course, which he probably would not want to, having already been trained to do the job he wanted in the first place.

Some examples of jobs

Look at the job advertisements on page 155.

Suggested work

Using the advertisements, answer the following questions:
1   Which jobs would it be suitable for a school leaver to apply for?

2   Which firms are looking for workers in the construction industry?

3   Several firms require people with driving licences. Which are they, and why in each case do you think the licence is required?

4   Look at the advertisement for an 'Estimator'. What industry is this job in? What do you think the job would involve?

5   Can you find any jobs which would be in Group VI?

How to get a job

Looking at advertisements is only one way to get a job, and is not always the best way. Other ways include asking your relatives and neighbours if they know of any vacancies in their own firms, going to the Careers Office (if you are under 18 and have never had a full-time job) or Jobcentre, or 'Knocking'. 'Knocking' means going round firms in person, asking for the Personnel Manager, or in a small place the Manager, and asking if they have any vacancies. You will have noticed how many of the job advertisements you looked at asked for 'smart' or 'well-spoken' applicants, so it is best to be well dressed and very polite. Many firms will not require staff but some people have found a job in this way.

You should have had plenty of practice elsewhere in writing letters of application, but you might like to have a go at writing an imaginary letter applying for one of the jobs in the advertisements. Remember that a firm will decide by looking at your letter whether they are going to call you for an interview, so it is very important to impress them. Tell them about your past experience (part-time work, holiday jobs, work experience), your qualifications, the qualifications you are studying for at the moment, your age, and any special skills or interests you have.

If you go for an interview, remember that you are one of many, and have to persuade the firm you are just what they are looking for. Could you answer these questions?

When you get a job

'A fair day's work for a fair day's pay'
Having a job is a two-way business. You are expected to work to the best of your ability and the firm is expected to treat you properly and pay you what they have promised. Working benefits you, through your pay, and it benefits your employer, through the work you do. The expression 'a fair day's work for a fair day's pay' means that both parties – you and the firm – should stick by their side of the bargain. This bargain is in fact a *legal contract* both you and your employer enter into when you start work. The terms of the contract are written down in your *contract of employment* which your employer must give you within 13 weeks of your starting work. It should set out the basic terms of your employment – your duties, your hours, and your pay, but may be fairly general, referring to 'accepted custom or practice' or 'agreed wage rates current at the time' and similar phrases. Important points it will answer are:

Can I be forced to work overtime? (If it doesn't say so, you can't be.)
How much holiday do I get?
Can I take another job at the same time? (This is not allowed in any case where the second job would interfere with the first, or when you are going to work for one of your firm's competitors.) Taking a second job is called *moonlighting*.

Most of your rights and duties at work are not set out in your contract of employment though; they apply whatever your contract says.

Your duties at work

You must give *faithful service*. This means you must not steal from your employer, be careless or incompetent, take bribes, give away the firm's secrets, or refuse to work, like by going on strike or going slow.

You must also obey all reasonable orders, providing these are lawful (you can't be ordered to do something illegal) and are in accordance with your contract of employment and other *terms and conditions* of your service.

Your rights at work

Providing you fulfill your duties, your employer must pay you the agreed sum. And he or she must pay you in money. In the 'bad old days' factory owners would pay their workers in the form of a Truck, or *Credit note*. This could be used to buy goods, but only from the firm's shop. You can guess that the goods in the shop were of poor quality and expensive. Eventually the Truck Acts were passed, making this practice illegal.

What if the firm cannot afford to pay you? Then they must, by law, go into liquidation, which means their machinery and land will be sold off, and the money used, first of all, to pay what you are owed.

You also have some other basic rights.

Sex and race discrimination

You cannot be treated or paid in any worse way because of your race or sex. Employers are not allowed to pay men and women different amounts for doing what is more or less the same job, unless they employ five or fewer people.

CASE HISTORY: Mr Smith and Mrs White were both drivers for a large company, Mr Smith in the transport department, Mrs White in catering. Mr Smith sometimes drove on public roads, whereas Mrs White only drove around the factory, and Mr Smith was paid more. Mrs White claimed Equal Pay — and won. The difference in the jobs did not justify different pay rates.

In general, firms cannot take race or sex into account when deciding who to employ either, nor can they advertise a job so that only men, or only women, or only black people can apply.

Illegal adverts

Wanted: Pretty Typist. (discriminates against men)	Wanted: Irish Navvies. (discriminates against non-Irish)
Wanted: Labourers; must be over six feet tall and have beards (discriminates against women).	Wanted: Machine operators – must have English grandparents (discriminates against non-English).

There are exceptions, though, if the job *genuinely requires* a particular sex or race to do it, or if the job involves national security, or is in the police force, prison service, church, mining or midwifery.

Legal adverts

Wanted: Drummer for Reggae band; must be black	Wanted: Lavatory Attendant – must be female for Ladies lavatory
Wanted: Man to play 'Othello' in forthcoming production	Wanted: Waiter in Chinese restaurant – Chinese only need apply
Wanted: Civil servant to work in Ministry of Defence – must be British	Wanted: Pool attendant for male changing rooms – men only need apply

It *is* legal to ask for, or refuse, people of a particular *religion* (except between Catholics and Protestants in Northern Ireland), and where the job is doing domestic work in a private household.

Trade union activity

An employer can refuse to employ trade union members, but once you are employed in a job, you cannot be prevented from joining, or trying to join, a union. You also cannot be prevented from taking part in trade union activities, providing these take place outside working hours.

You also have the right *not* to join a trade union, unless your firm has a *closed shop* agreement (see page 170).

Pregnancy – All pregnant women have the right to take time off work to go to ante-natal classes and providing they have worked for the firm for at least 104 weeks, they have the right to 6 weeks maternity pay, and to return to their old job after the baby is born. (This does not apply if there are five or less employees.)

Holidays – You have no rights to any holidays at all unless your contract says so.

Pay slip – You have a right to an 'itemised pay statement' saying how your wages were worked out, and what any deductions were for.

Losing your job

You can be sacked if you do not fulfill your *duties at work*. Usually you must be given at least one warning first, probably in writing. For very serious misbehaviour (ie gross misconduct) you can be sacked, or dismissed *instantly*, but more often you will be given notice. The minimum period of notice is one week.

You cannot be sacked for taking part in trade union activity, or because of your sex or race, from the moment you start work. And once you have worked for an employer for six months you are entitled to a written statement saying why you were sacked. After a year (2 years for firms with less than 20 employees) you are protected against being sacked *unfairly*. In other words, your breach of your duties must be serious enough to make it reasonable for you to be sacked.

Suppose you are sacked unfairly?

You take your case to an Industrial Tribunal. You must do this within three months, and you do it by completing a form available from your union or a Jobcentre. Unless your claim is about Sex or Racial Discrimination, you must have been employed for a year. Your case will be decided by a Tribunal. They can order:

1 Your employer to give you your job back, and, or
2 Award you compensation up to £6250, depending on your age, and how long you have worked for the firm.

If they order your firm to give you your job back and they won't, the Tribunal can double the award.

Note that if your employer operates a closed shop, and you lose your job because the union expels you, or won't let you join, you can still claim unfair dismissal.

You can get free advice on sex discrimination and racial matters from the Equal Opportunities Commission, and the Commission for Racial Equality – see 'phone book.

Constructive dismissal

If you are forced to resign, either directly ('Resign or be sacked!'), or because your employer has broken your contract of employment, you can still claim unfair dismissal, even though you left of your own accord.

Redundancy

It may be that you are sacked because your firm no longer needs you. This is called being made redundant. If you have worked for a firm for two years or more you are entitled to a special payment – called Redundancy Pay – if this happens, but you cannot claim unfair dismissal, unless you have been singled out unfairly for redundancy. For instance a firm could not make all its black workers redundant, or all its trade union members redundant. Similarly, you can be sacked for going on strike (because you are not fulfilling your duties at work), but it would be unfair if a firm singled out a few workers from everyone who went on strike for dismissal.

And don't forget – the duties in the Health and Safety at Work Act (see Chapter 3) are legal duties. If you break them you could be sacked. And if your employer breaks them you could leave and claim constructive dismissal.

Suggested work

1   What different ways are there to look for a job?

2   What advice would you give a friend who was going to be interviewed for a job?

3   How long must you work in a job before you can demand a contract of employment?

4   What are your 'duties at work'?

5   Which of the following advertisements are illegal, and why?
    A. Wanted: Typist – must wear a skirt
    B. Wanted: Midwife – must be female
    C. Wanted: Actress to play 'Ophelia' in forthcoming production – must be female

D. Wanted: Drivers — must have beards

E. Wanted for Indian Restaurant — waiters; must be Indian

F. Wanted: Undercover agent to join Foreign Service — must be British

6 What would you do if you were sacked for joining a trade union?

7 What is 'Constructive Dismissal'?

8 Fred Jones works for a small firm employing 18 people. He has been sacked for refusing to work overtime. He has been employed for 18 months and was never told that overtime was compulsory. Can he do anything about it?

9 Are the following statements true or false:

A. Everyone is entitled to at least two weeks' holiday per year.

B. You do not get any redundancy pay until you have worked for a firm for over two years.

C. It is quite in order for a firm to pay you with a credit note.

D. You cannot be sacked for going on strike.

E. You can be sacked for breaking safety rules.

You and your pay

Four different firms want workers to pack oranges in crates. Which pays the most?

FIRM A: £97.50 per week

FIRM B: £1.75 per hour

FIRM C: £1.05 per hour, plus 45p per box packed

FIRM D: £65 per week, plus bonus of £34.50 if 80 boxes per week completed

Answer? You can't tell. They all work out their pay in different ways. You can't even tell which of the first two pays the most, because you do not know how many hours per week the job is for.

Fixed rate pay

This is worked out according to *how long* you work for. Both firms A and B above operate fixed pay schemes. Pay can be so much an hour, week, month or year. *Wages* are usually worked out at so much an hour. The *basic rate* will apply to the normal week without overtime, which is usually 35, 39 or 40 hours. Any time more than this will usually be paid at a higher, *overtime* rate, often 'time and a half'. 'Time and a half' means the basic rate, plus half as much again. So basic rate £2.50 an hour gives 'time and a half' of £3.75 an hour. 'Double time' would be £5.00 an hour, and so on.

What would the following amounts of pay work out to:

40 hours @ £2.50 plus 5 hours overtime @ time and a half

35 hours @ £1.75 plus 8 hours overtime @ time and a half
39 hours @ £2.25 plus 4 hours overtime @ double time

Sometimes, in addition to the basic pay, an extra amount is payable for each piece of work done. This is called *piecework* and was operated by Firm C.
Advantages: Encourages workers to work quickly
Disadvantages: Leads to poor quality when work is rushed, and arguments about whether a particular piece is good enough or not. Requires careful quality control, and a lot of time adding up bits of work.
Try this one: Basic pay £1.05 per hour, plus 45p per box of oranges packed. Jean packed 85 boxes in the 40 hours, Mary packed 74 boxes. How much did they each earn?

In an effort to get over the disadvantages of piecework, but still encourage people to work quickly, many firms have now introduced *bonus work*, or *measured day work*. With this system, workers are set a target of how much work they are expected to do in the day or week. If they reach the target, they get a bonus. Firm D worked this method.
Advantages: Encourages workers. Sometimes firms allow their workers to go home early when the target is reached. It is popular with workers and much easier for firms to work out than piecework. It is suitable for many jobs, from making screws to emptying dustbins.
Disadvantages: Leads to arguments about what the target should be. If it's too low, it is always reached and does not act as an encouragement. If it's too high the workers will rarely get the bonus. And what do you do if the machines break down?
Note: 'Flexi-time' means that the hours of work can be varied to suit the employee. So long as 35 (say) hours a week are worked, the employee can start anytime between 8 and 10, and finish anytime between 3 and 5, or whatever times the firm decides. Not really suitable for a factory because the machinery often has to be started at a particular time, but quite popular in offices.

Salary

Whereas wages are worked out by the hour, a *salary* is usually given as a yearly amount, and is paid in twelve equal instalments, one each month. Jobs which pay salaries frequently do not allow overtime, or do not pay for overtime when it is worked. The idea is that a person on a salary is paid to do a job, however long that might take, rather than being paid for a fixed length of time. In practice most people on salaries do have set hours of work though.

More sums

Which is more: £85 per week or £4500 per annum (year)?

How much per month is a salary of £6400 per annum?
How much per annum would a wage of £3.50 an hour be, if the employee worked 40 hours per week?

Commission

A *commission* is a percentage of the money a salesman or woman takes, paid as part of wages or salary. Shop assistants may be paid a commission on everything they sell. The commission can be a major part of a salesman's earnings.

Advantage: The more the person sells, the more they earn
Disadvantage: The person's pay will vary from week to week or month to month, sometimes by a lot, and will go down dramatically if he or she is ill or on holiday (though some firms allow for this).

How it's paid

Most people in Britain receive their wages each week in cash. The *pay packet* contains a statement giving the pay and deductions, and a collection of appropriate notes and coins. Although this is popular with many people, it is not a very sensible system, and is very unusual in America and on the Continent, for example. It leads to large amounts of money being carried around (sometimes hundreds of thousands of pounds) which encourages robberies and losses. It requires a big cash office with people counting out the wages, and a lot of it ends up back in a bank, possibly even the same bank it came from.

Alternatives to the wage packet

Many people are nowadays paid by cheque instead of cash. This means that they need a bank account of course, but it avoids large sums of cash being in transit between the bank and the firm, and large sums being in people's pockets. It does mean that people *have* to go to the bank though, to pay in their cheque, and that they have to draw money out of the bank when they want to spend it.

To make the system even easier, some firms pay wages by *credit transfer*. The employee receives a slip which says: 'The following amount has been credited to your bank account . . . . . .'. This saves the employee having to go to the bank to pay the cheque in.

Most people receiving salaries are paid by credit transfer, because the amounts of money involved are so large, most salaries being paid monthly, and therefore containing just over four times as much as an equivalent weekly pay packet.

Further questions

1   Look back to the page of job advertisements earlier in this chapter. Can you find examples of the following:
   a) salary scales (yearly)
   b) wage rates (weekly or hourly)
   c) commission payments
   d) a job with bonus payments

2   What is meant by piecework?

3   What is measured day work? What arrangement do you think a firm should make to cover the machines' breaking down?

4   What would be the advantages of getting paid weekly, and of getting paid monthly?

5   Why is it a good idea for wages and salaries to be paid by credit transfer? How could you persuade people to accept this, and why do you think they might object?

How much pay?

Different people are paid vastly different amounts of money for the work they do. One of the job advertisements asked for a Sales Assistant and was offering £50 per week. And yet there are some people at the very top in industry who can earn this amount every hour. Not many, it is true. Even the Prime Minister earns less than that. But quite a lot of people earn £50 a day. What accounts for these differences?

First, age. Young people, particularly those under 18, do not earn as much as adults. Often they are still training, and can see their pay increase as they become more skilled and qualified.

Secondly, training whatever your age. If jobs requiring high qualifications and skills did not offer more money, people might not be prepared to spend the time and effort learning the skills.

Thirdly, demand. If there is a shortage of a particular type of worker, then firms will have to offer more money to attract people into the job. The easier a job is to do, broadly speaking the less pay it will attract, since there will be more people who could do it. That is why top footballers and pop stars earn so much — they are in possession of very special and rare skills.

Remember the work you did on the structure of firms in chapter 2? We saw then that people in more responsible jobs are paid more to attract the best people into those jobs. The decisions a Managing Director makes might affect the livelihood of hundreds of workers, so it is important to get the best person available to make the decisions. And the decisions a doctor makes could save or damage a life. So responsibility is important in affecting pay.

Some jobs are more dangerous or unpleasant than others, and these jobs are often paid more (but not always — it also depends how difficult they are). And some jobs are considered more valuable to the community, and are therefore more highly paid. (But remember what we saw earlier in this chapter — all jobs are valuable in one way or another.)

So age, skills, qualifications, length of training, demand, responsibility, and perhaps danger and value to the community all affect how much a job is paid. They also affect a job's *status*, which means how highly people judge it. Doctor and Bank manager are two high status jobs — highly regarded by people in general. Remember that no one has ever sat down and decided how much every job should be paid. The differences have just come about over the years. And the differences are getting smaller. Over the past forty years many of the lower paid jobs have increased their pay far more than the more highly paid jobs. A solicitor is now paid less, in real terms, than he or she was in 1940, whereas an engine driver and a farm labourer are both paid over twice as much in real terms as in 1940. ('In real terms' means taking inflation into account and looking at what a certain amount of money would have bought in 1940, compared with what the new amount would buy today.)

How much are they worth?

Look at this list of jobs:
air line pilot, judge, road-sweeper, teacher, doctor, nurse, barman/woman, bus driver, motor mechanic, civil engineer.

1 Arrange them in order, from 1 to 10, according to how much you think each one should be paid, taking into account the things listed above, like age, qualifications, etc.
2 Now, in groups of three or four, try and compile an agreed order between you. Make sure it is agreed — no majority voting; if one of you disagrees try and persuade him or her why he or she should change his or her opinion — or listen to the arguments and change yours!
3 Were you right? Find out from your Careers library how much the average pay is for each of these jobs.

166

Trade unions

One of the decisions everyone has to take when starting a job is whether or not they should join a trade union. What will they get out of it? What are unions for? A vital defence for the worker against unscrupulous bosses; or an old-fashioned system holding back productivity and flying in the face of personal freedom?

'Everyone out!'

Hardly a day seems to go by without the newspapers or television mentioning a strike of workers in one firm or another. Sometimes such a strike has a dramatic effect on people, like stopping the buses or trains running, causing power cuts, or closing the schools. More often a strike affects few people directly, other than those involved with the firm concerned. People who are not on strike are often quick to blame the trade unions for any loss or inconvenience they suffer.

This is rather a one-sided view of unions, however. Strikes get reported because they are newsworthy, but there are not nearly as many of them as one might imagine. In fact, in a normal *year*, the average time lost through strikes is *under an hour* for each worker. This is far, far less than the time lost through other causes, like illness.

Working normally: 11 months, 30 days, 7 hours, 10 minutes	On strike: 50 minutes

And many millions of workers have never been on strike at all in their whole working lives.

What is a strike?

A strike is when a group of workers refuse to work, either because they are unhappy with their pay or conditions, or because they feel the management of the firm has been acting very unfairly. When workers are on strike, their firm does not pay them any wages, so they lose their pay.

Also, since nothing is being made, the firm loses money too. And if the business is one used by members of the public (like the buses), they will suffer loss and inconvenience as well. So everyone loses during a strike, which is why going on strike is a last resort, and rather rare. Because of this, trade unions try and avoid strikes. Most strikes are 'unofficial', or 'widcat', which means they are not supported by the union.

But occasionally, the union will agree that a strike is the only way left to solve a problem, or dispute, and the strike then becomes 'official', and the union gives its members who are on strike a small amount of strike pay. Note that people who are on strike cannot claim any money for themselves from the Department of Health and Social Security, only for their families.

So what do unions do?

They negotiate. A union is an organization of workers, either in one particular industry, or across a group of different industries. The workers each pay a small subscription and the union then employs *officials* to talk to the employers on the workers' behalf. These officials are skilled at sorting out problems, and save workers having to disagree with their own employer. They talk about wages, holidays, conditions at work (whether a factory is too hot or too cold, or an office too crowded), safety and training. They offer their members advice about compensation for accidents or sickness, and before the state retirement pension came into being they used to pay pensions to retired workers, or workers' dependents.

Because the union official represents a lot of people, he or she has a lot more influence with the firm than a single worker.

Grievance procedure

Most unions have agreed with their firm a set procedure to be followed if there is a dispute. This procedure is called the *grievance procedure*, and works something like this:

Tom Brown has a complaint about a change being made in the shifts he is working. First he will see his immediate supervisor (perhaps the foreman). If this does not resolve the problem he may go to the Personnel Manager. If he is still unhappy he will discuss the matter with his Union, who will approach the Personnel Manager on his behalf. The Union will be likely to know if he has a good case, and will know if any other people have similar problems.

The main point about a Grievance Procedure is that many problems can be sorted out at an early stage if the procedure is followed.

The shop steward

Often the members of a union in one particular firm will elect one of their number to be their shop steward. He or she will represent their views to the management of the firm about minor matters which can be dealt with without the need for a union official.

Why strike?

Very occasionally, the negotiations break down when the union officials and the management of the firm simply cannot agree, perhaps about a pay claim. There is then very little the workers can do except take *industrial action* to try and persuade the firm to change its mind. Even at this point there is a way out, though.

There is an independent body called ACAS (the Advisory Conciliation and Arbitration Service) which, if both parties ask, will look into a dispute and suggest a compromise. You many have heard the expression 'going to arbitration'.

Industrial action is much more likely if the workers do not trust the management, or the management will not negotiate at all, and some firms over the years fall into a pattern of mutual mistrust and consequent industrial action.

Industrial action

The *go-slow*. This is where workers do their normal job, but do it much more slowly than usual, so less is produced. It is similar to the *work-to-rule* where the workers follow every little rule to the letter, thereby taking much longer than usual to do everything. Also used is the *overtime ban*, when workers refuse to work any longer than their standard (usually eight hour) day. And finally, there is the *strike*.

Too much power?

Unions only have the power their members give them — they are groups of ordinary people. And very few people in this country would say that workers should not be able to strike if they are very unhappy with their firm; after all striking is a last resort, and the workers themselves lose money by it as well as the firm. Certainly the union gives a worker far more power than he or she would have on his or her own, but by doing so it protects the worker from the whim of an unscrupulous or mean employer.

But there are some ways in which unions can have power over people who have nothing to do with them or the firm they work for.

1 Political power

Although ten million people are members of trade unions, this is less than half the workforce, and only a fifth of the country as a whole. Yet the unions have a very big say in the policies of the Labour Party, and hence the government when Labour is in power. This is because the unions pay most of the Labour Party's expenses, through the *policital levy* which most union members pay as part of their subscription. Members do not have to pay this levy, but many of them do not know this.

Some people think it is unfair that relatively few people should have this large say, but others think that it is right that the views of ordinary working people should be represented in government policy in this way. It is also true that many union members who complain about the political power of the unions do not themselves attend union meetings and help to form the policies.

2 Power over the public

Some workers in 'key' industries (like electricity generation) can cause immense harm to people who have nothing to do with the dispute when they strike. A very few workers (like the police) are not allowed to go on strike for this reason, but some people think many more should be included, perhaps hospital workers, miners, and power workers. On the other hand, what would these workers then do if they did have a serious grievance?

3 Picketting

Picketting is when a group of workers on strike forms up outside the factory gates and tries to persuade the other workers to go on strike too. If a union member refuses, he or she is called a *blackleg*. So long as the picket is peaceful this is quite legal and acceptable, but sometimes the strikers picket other factories (perhaps their firm's supplier or customer) and try and stop their workers working. This is called *secondary picketting*, and some people think it is unfair both on the other firm and its workers.

4 The closed shop

In a 'closed shop' all the workers in a particular place of employment have to belong to a union if they are to keep their job. This is an agreement between the union and the firm. The argument in favour of closed shops is that everyone benefits from the union's negotiations, so everyone should support the union. On the other hand, perhaps people should be free to decide whether they want to join the union or not.

The law and unions

During the 19th century people fought long and hard to win the right to strike and form unions, sometimes being sent to prison for their pains. The result is that unions have a special place in the law, and firms now have to give a fair deal to their workers in terms of pay and conditions. Opinion changes about whether some of the unions' powers are right or wrong, however, and governments periodically pass laws over such matters as those raised above. In many countries it is still illegal to belong to a union or to go on strike, whatever the reason, such as in some of the South American countries, and until recently even in Spain and Greece.

The TUC

Each year representatives of the different unions meet together in the Trade Union Congress to discuss matters which concern them all. Throughout the year the TUC sorts out problems between unions, and represents the union point of view to the government.

Things to do

1   What is a trade union?

2   What is the difference between a shop steward and a union official?

3   Imagine you are a shop steward, and have been asked by your fellow union members to go and see the personnel manager and ask for an extra week's holiday for everyone this year. What arguments might you use to support the claim?
    If you were the personnel manager, what arguments might you use to persuade the shop steward that the extra holiday was not a good idea?

4   What different forms of industrial action are there?

5   What do you think of: closed shops; secondary picketting; forbidding certain groups of workers to go on strike? (Who would you include?)

6   The *five* biggest unions are the TGWU, the AUEW, the GMWU, NALGO and NUPE. Can you find out what each of these initials stands for, and what types of workers each represents?

Sample multiple choice questions

1   The purpose of a grievance procedure is to settle disputes between

a) customers and a firm
b) shareholders and managers
c) a firm and its suppliers
d) workers and management

2 The shop steward is
a) elected by a group of workers to represent them
b) appointed by the firm to represent the workforce
c) a full-time union official
d) a worker chosen by the union to represent the workforce

3 'Block release' means that a trainee will
a) go to a College of Further Education one day per week
b) work for a number of different firms
c) go to a College of Further Education for a period of several months
d) be trained entirely on the firm's premises

4 A demarcation dispute is a disagreement about
a) who should do a particular job
b) which union should speak for the workforce
c) piece work rates
d) the length of time taken over training

5 A craftsman is
a) a skilled worker who has served an apprenticeship
b) a semi-skilled worker who has been trained by the firm
c) an unskilled worker
d) a professional

6 Which of the following groups contains only skilled jobs?
a) plasterer, machine operator, turner
b) fitter, mechanic, barman
c) plasterer, fitter, mechanic
d) joiner, barman, bricklayer

7 Being paid on 'piecework' means
a) paid a yearly salary divided into twelve pieces paid monthly
b) paid a basic wage with a bonus for completing a target
c) paid commission on sales
d) paid a basic wage with an extra amount for each item produced

8 A 'closed shop' agreement means
a) no more workers will be taken on
b) everyone must be a member of a trade union
c) the hours of work are fixed
d) no one in the firm belongs to a trade union

9 A firm may not take a person's sex into account when offering a job unless
a) the person is a member of a trade union

b) they have a preference for a man or a woman
c) the firm has less than 20 workers
d) the firm has less than 5 employees

10 Which of the following organizations negotiates by collective bargaining?
a) an Industrial Training Board
b) a trade union
c) the Department of Employment
d) the Confederation of British Industry

11 When a person's pay is increased according to how much he or she sells, he or she is said to be paid
a) a bonus
b) on piecework
c) commission
d) a profit share

12 Young people are required to attend school from the ages of
a) 4−15.
b) 4−16.
c) 5−16.
d) 5−18.

13 Social mobility describes
a) people moving house to get a job
b) people moving up or down the social scale
c) people being provided with free transport
d) people being given free transport to work

14 Moonlighting means
a) working a night shift
b) working out of doors
c) taking a second job
d) working while drawing unemployment pay

15 Which of the following would *not* be a fair reason for dismissal?
a) going on strike
b) incompetence
c) theft from the employer
d) joining a union

9

Society at work

National government

Britain is governed from the Houses of Parliament in Westminster, London. You may well have been to the Houses of Parliament, or Palace of Westminster, as they are sometimes called, and will certainly have seen pictures of them. You will remember the clock tower with 'Big Ben'.

It is Parliament which makes the laws which control our lives, and which supervises the way these laws are put into effect. Parliament is made up of three parts: the House of Commons, the House of Lords, and the Queen. The Queen is the head of Parliament in the sense that it is her Parliament which governs her country, and she has to approve everything that it does, but in practice nowadays, and indeed for the past three hundred years, the monarch has little more than ceremonial duties to perform. The work of Parliament is carried out by the Houses of Commons and Lords (that is why we speak of the Houses, and not the House, of Parliament). The House of Commons consists of 635 elected representatives of the people of this country; the House of Lords contains over 1000 'peers'. A peer is a person with a title, like Lord or Duke, which they have either inherited from their father, or been awarded for outstanding service to the public or the government. All titles awarded since 1965 have been 'life peerages'; that is to say the holder keeps his or her title until death, but it is not passed on to the oldest child, or inherited. The senior bishops and the Law Lords also sit in the House of Lords.

Laws connected with money are only discussed by the House of Commons, but all other laws have to be discussed by both Commons and Lords. The House of Lords cannot refuse to pass a law the House of Commons wants, though it can delay the law for a maximum of one year.

How laws are made

Any member of the House of Commons can propose a law, providing he or she can get the time to do so. The proposed law, which is called a *Bill*, is read to the House. This is called the first reading. Those members who are present in the House at the time then vote to decide whether they wish the bill to go any further. If so, then the bill is written out and circulated to give members a chance to consider it. It is then read out again, some time later – the second reading. Again, those members present vote on whether they wish the bill to proceed, and if so, the bill is examined by a small committee of members. This committee looks for possible faults in the bill, unforeseen difficulties, and ways of improving it. They decide on a final wording for the bill (this is very important since what the bill says may become the law), and then take the results back to the House for the third reading. This time, the members present make their final decision on whether to accept the bill or not. If they vote to accept it, the bill is sent to the House of Lords for discussion (unless it is a bill connected with money – a *finance* bill). The Lords can suggest improvements (called *amendments*) or reject the bill altogether. As already mentioned, if they reject the bill, the House of Commons can send it to them again a year later and they have no choice but to accept it then. If the Lords do accept the bill, then it is sent to the Queen for approval. Once she has signed it, or given the *Royal Assent*, the bill is called an Act of Parliament, and is law. It is many years since a monarch refused to sign a bill, and our present Queen never has. It is most unlikely she ever would, unless the House of Commons voted to abolish elections, or something of that sort.

The real importance of the monarchy is that it is there just in case. The fact that the Queen has to agree to all laws prevents any real abuse of power arising. And the Queen's power is theoretically backed up by the fact that she is the head of the Courts of Law, the Police and the Armed Services. If the Queen ordered the Army to do one thing, and the House of Commons ordered them to do another, we do not know what would happen: quite possibly they would obey the Queen, but the situation last arose three hundred years ago, and on that occasion led to the Civil War, when half obeyed the monarch and the other half Parliament.

As well as passing laws, Parliament has to see that they are put into effect. This is done by the Civil Service, which is arranged into departments, each department looking after a different piece of Parliament's work.

The government

Most members of Parliament belong to a political party. The party with the largest number of members more or less controls Parliament, since they can vote for most of the laws they want. This controlling party forms the *government*, and elects one of its members to be Prime Minister. The Prime Minister then chooses members of the House of Commons or Lords to head each of the government departments. They are called Secretaries of State, and there is one in charge of the Home Office (the Home Secretary), the Foreign Office (the Foreign Secretary), the Departments of the Environment, Health and Social Security, Education and Science, the Treasury (the Chancellor of the Exchequer), and so on. These Secretaries of State together make up the *Cabinet*.

In the large departments, there are also *Ministers* appointed to look after parts of the department's work. There is, for example, a Minister of

Defence in the Foreign Office, and a Minister of Transport in the Department of the Environment. These Secretaries of State and Ministers are responsible for what the civil servants in their departments do, and can be questioned by other members of the House about their actions. The Prime Minister also can be questioned about her actions, and you may have heard Prime Minister's question time on the radio.

The opposition

The second largest party in the House of Commons forms the opposition. They watch what the government does, and usually vote against the government's proposals. If the government loses an important vote (this usually means members of the government party must have voted with the opposition) then they may be forced to resign, resulting in a general election.

The speaker

Because the House of Commons works like a large committee, with debates, proposals, and voting, it needs a Chairman to keep order, and to tell people when they can speak. The Chairman of the House of Commons is called the Speaker. He takes no part in debates, but does have a casting vote if there is a draw on an issue. Unlike other Chairmen, though, he always votes *against* any new proposal, whoever is making it.

The members of parliament

Because Britain is a democracy, every adult has the right to vote for the person who will represent them in Parliament. And everyone also has the right to stand for election to Parliament if he or she wishes. Britain is divided into 635 *constituencies*, each of which is represented by one member of Parliament, its MP. It should be noted that the MP represents *all* the people in that constituency, not just those who voted. The only way anyone can tell who you voted for in an election is by asking you, and of course you do not have to say. The boundaries of each constituency, and the number of constituencies there are change from time to time in an attempt to keep each constituency roughly the same size.

Each constituency has a list of the names of people who are entitled to vote in an election. This is called the *electoral roll*, and if you are not on this roll, even though you may be entitled to vote in other respects, you cannot vote. Once each year the roll is updated by asking each householder to list those people in his household who are over 18, or who will become 18 during the following year, who are not certified insane or in prison. When the roll is published, those people who are not yet 18, but will become 18 during the year, are marked as Young Voters, and can vote on or after their 18th birthday. To be able to vote, you must be both over 18, *and* on the electoral roll. Before any election, those people on the roll are sent a card telling them where to vote; called the polling station.

176

If you move house during the year, or go to live away from home, you will not be on the electoral roll in your new area. However you can still vote in your old area, by asking for a *postal vote*. You make your vote in exactly the same way as you would at the Polling Station, only you post it in. You can apply to the Returning or Registration Officer at your local council for a postal vote.

The ballot paper

When you go to make your vote, you will be given a ballot paper giving the names of all the people standing for election in your constituency. Anyone over the age of 21 can stand, providing they put forward the deposit of £150. If a candidate receives less than 15% of the total vote, he or she loses this deposit. Most candidates are members of a political party, and this is stated on the ballot paper.

BROWN, Angela Mary	Labour Party	
GREEN, Thomas	Conservative Party	
WILKINS, Frederick	Independent	X
WILLIS, Mary Anne	Liberal Party	

You vote by placing a cross by the name of the candidate you support, folding your ballot paper, and placing it in the tin provided. When the poll closes, all the boxes are taken from the polling station to a central place, and the votes are counted, under the eyes of all the candidates. The candidate with most votes wins. If the result is close, one of the candidates can ask for a *recount*, but in the end only one vote is sufficient to decide the election. The number of votes that a candidate wins by is called a *majority*.

The government can resign, and call a General Election in every constituency, whenever it likes, but it must do so at least once every five years. Between times there might be an election in just one constituency, though, if the MP resigns, or dies. This type of election is called a by-election, but is identical to any other election in every respect.

Changes in the system

In some ways the system we use to elect MP's is rather unfair. In an extreme case a party could come second in every constituency in the country and end up with millions of votes, but no MP's. The reason we use our system is that traditionally we have been represented by a person, not by a party. Nowadays we generally vote according to a candidate's party, though, and so many people think it would be more sensible to have a system which resulted in the number of MP's of each party in the House of Commons reflecting the total votes given throughout the country to that party. It is possible to compromise between these two systems by grouping constituencies together, say four at a time, and allowing people to vote for four candidates in order of preference. The four MP's elected to represent the four constituencies would then reflect people's second, third and fourth choices, as well as their first. This is called *proportional representation*, and is supported by the Liberal and Social Democratic Parties.

Local government.

Many aspects of our daily lives are controlled not by the government, but by our local councils. They have responsibility for education, local roads, housing, transport, environmental health, the fire and police services, and leisure facilities. The government often lays down rules local councils have to follow, but they are allowed to make many decisions on their own. The decisions are taken by local councillors, who are elected in the same way as MP's. Being a local councillor is not a full-time job, and local councillors are not paid (as are MP's) although they receive an allowance for the work they do.

Each constituency is divided into *wards*, and each ward has its own councillor. There are two levels of local government, the County, Metropolitan, or Regional Councils, and the Borough or District Councils, and the activities they control are divided between them. There are separate elections for each type of council.

178

Suggested work

1 What are the *three* sections of Parliament?

2 What type of laws do not have to go before the House of Lords?

3 What is a 'life peer'? What is an hereditary peer?

4 Describe the progress of a bill through Parliament, from when it is first proposed to when it becomes a law?

5 What is a general election? What is the maximum time a government can run without calling a general election?

6 Do you know the names of the present members of the Cabinet? Who is the Home Secretary, the Foreign Secretary, the Chancellor of the Exchequer?

7 What is the electoral roll? How do you get your name on the electoral roll?

8 Why do some people think that proportional representation would be a good idea?

9 Who is your local County or Regional councillor? And your District or Borough councillor? And your MP?

10 For your area, find out which activities are the responsibility of each level of local government (it varies according to whether you live in a County or Metropolitan County, London or a Scottish Region).

We all use schools, doctors, hospitals and the roads. The country has an Army, Navy and Air Force to protect it, and a police force to uphold the law. Each house has its dustbins emptied, is connected to the water supply and, in most cases, to the drainage system. People who have retired or are too sick to work collect pensions, and parents receive child benefit each month for their children.

In most cases these services are provided free of charge, but they still cost money. Some are paid for by the government, and some by local authorities, and the money to provide them comes from the money we

179

pay in rates and taxes. Altogether they add up to an enormous amount of money. In fact, just about half of all the money spent in Britain is spent by government and local authorities.

Tax

Tax is money paid by people to the government, and falls into two groups. *Direct* tax is tax paid out of what we earn, usually before we get paid, and *indirect* tax is tax paid on things we buy. There are two main direct taxes, income tax and National Insurance.

Income tax

A person is charged income tax on what he or she earns, wherever it comes from, at a basic rate of 30 pence in the pound (30%). But you do not pay income tax on all your earnings. You are allowed to earn a certain amount (called your *allowances*) before you pay tax. The allowances for a single person for 1983 are £1785 (£35 per week), and for a married couple £2795 (£52 per week).

To work out how much tax you will pay each week, take your allowances off your total pay (called your *gross* pay) and multiply the number of pounds left by 30p each.

Complications

In practice, your employer deducts your tax each time you are paid, and sends the money to the Inland Revenue. You have a *code number* which shows what your allowances are and by looking at tax tables the amount of tax due can be calculated. Your yearly allowances are ten times your code number, so with a single person's allowances your code number will be 178. Since your allowances are spread over the tax year, which runs from 6 April to the next 5 April, if you do not work all of this time you will pay less tax when you do work to compensate. This method of tax collection is PAYE (Pay As You Earn). The amount of tax a person pays goes up to 40p in the pound if they earn over £12 800 a year, and continues to rise for higher earners. Your allowances can alter according to your circumstances, which is why you fill in a *tax return* each year. The basic allowances and the rate of tax can change each year, usually in the Budget.

Example of income tax
Gross Pay: £70.45
Take off allowances: £70.45 − £35 = £35.45
Multiply number of pounds left by 30p = 35 × 30p = £10.50
So you will pay £10.50 tax.

National insurance

Unlike income tax, there are no allowances for National Insurance. Everyone who earns more than £30 per week (1983 figure) pays 9% of all their pay in National Insurance. This, too, is deducted by the employer. There is a maximum amount a person can pay each week, however, which is currently £21.15. In our example above of gross weekly pay of £70.45, the National Insurance would be £70 × 9% = £6.30

GROSS PAY: £70.45
DEDUCTIONS:
  INCOME TAX: £10.50
  NI: £6.30
    TOTAL: £16.80
NET PAY (what you get): £53.65

Indirect taxes

The main taxes we pay on what we spend are VAT (Value Added Tax), and excise duties.

VAT is charged on most goods (but not food or children's clothing) and services, and is, in 1984, 15% of the price. It is usually included in the advertised price of goods in shops, but not for some services (like garage repair work). When comparing prices you should always make sure that the VAT is included.

Excise duties are extra taxes paid on some things on top of VAT. Alcohol and tobacco are the main items concerned.
You can see why these items can be bought much more cheaply at 'duty free' shops where there is no excise duty!

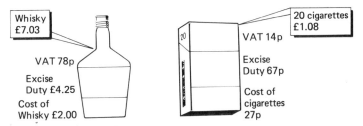

Special extra taxes are also paid when buying certain other goods, including cars, and petrol and oil. You will know there is also the *road fund tax* to pay when you own a car, currently £85 per year. This is the 'tax disc' on a car's windscreen.

Rates

Local authorities, being Metropolitan and County Councils, District and Borough, Regional and Islands Councils, pay for schools, housing, some roads, water, sewage, refuse disposal, parks, and towards the cost of the buses. Roughly half of their money comes in a grant — called the Rate Support Grant — from the government. The rest is paid for by the *rates*. Every house is given a *rateable value*, which reflects how much rent could be charged if the house was let to someone. It is more if the house has central heating, is bigger, has more rooms, and so on. The local authority works out how much money it needs to run the services, and then fixes a *rate*, which is the proportion of the rateable value each house will pay for the year. It is given as so much in every pound of rateable value.

Example of rates
Rateable value of house: £400
Rate for the year: 96p in the pound
Rates paid: 400 × 96p = £384

Many people think rates are an unfair tax. It is possible to get a *rebate*, which means being let off some of your rates if you have a low income, but apart from this rates are the only tax which takes no account of a person's ability to afford it. A person living on their own pays the same rates as a family of four wage earners living in a similar house next door. Firms, too, pay rates on all their buildings.

Company taxes

As well as rates, firms pay tax on their profits. This is called *corporation tax*. They also pay an extra *National Insurance* contribution for each of their employees, on top of what the employee pays, which is at the moment 13.2% of the wages.

Where the money comes from

Sources of central and local government revenue 1979:

Income tax and corporation tax:	£25 billion	
National Insurance:	£11½ billion	
VAT, excise duties and rates:	£30½ billion	Total £75 billion
Council house rents:	£2½ billion	
Various other taxes (betting duty, capital gains tax, land tax etc):	£5½ billion	

Source: National Income and Expenditure 1980

Where the money goes

Out of every £1 the government and local authorities spend, this much goes on:

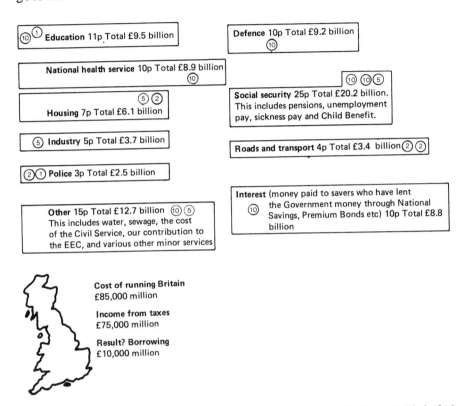

Education 11p Total £9.5 billion

Defence 10p Total £9.2 billion

National health service 10p Total £8.9 billion

Social security 25p Total £20.2 billion. This includes pensions, unemployment pay, sickness pay and Child Benefit.

Housing 7p Total £6.1 billion

Industry 5p Total £3.7 billion

Roads and transport 4p Total £3.4 billion

Police 3p Total £2.5 billion

Other 15p Total £12.7 billion This includes water, sewage, the cost of the Civil Service, our contribution to the EEC, and various other minor services

Interest (money paid to savers who have lent the Government money through National Savings, Premium Bonds etc) 10p Total £8.8 billion

Cost of running Britain £85,000 million

Income from taxes £75,000 million

Result? Borrowing £10,000 million

If you add the figures up, you will see they come to £85 billion. This is £10 billion more than the money raised from taxes, and the Government had to borrow the extra from savers to 'balance its books'.

Suggested work

1 What is meant by 'direct taxes'?

2 What are the *two* main direct taxes we pay?

3 What are 'indirect taxes'?

4 Give three examples of indirect taxes.

5 What are rates, and who are they paid to?

6 Draw a 'bar graph' showing the amounts of money the government and local authorities spend out of every pound on the various services they provide. Your vertical scale should go from 0 to 25p. Which service costs the most?

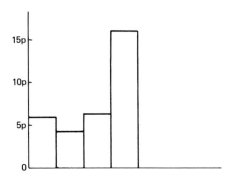

7   What is PAYE?

8   If you had to raise some extra money for the government (perhaps to cut down its borrowing) what taxes would you raise, and why?

9   Are there any taxes you would reduce or abolish because you think they are unfair?

10   Try and work out roughly how much your *net pay* would be (after deducting income tax and national insurance) if your *gross pay* was
a) £50 per week
b) £90 per week
c) £150 per week.

The social services

We have seen that government spending on Social Security accounts for almost a quarter of total spending, and is far and away the largest single item in the government's budget. This is because we live in a *Welfare State* where we believe that it is right and proper to provide money and services for people who either cannot work at all, or who work but do not earn very much.

Nowadays we take a great deal of this social security provision for granted, but it is only within the last forty years that the welfare state has grown up. Before the beginning of this century, if a family had no money, they either had to beg for charity, starve, or go to the workhouse, where they were separated and given menial work to do in return for very basic food. Then, at the start of the twentieth century, National Insurance was brought in, so that people at work could insure themselves against the day they had no work, or became too old for work. The worker, the employer, and the government each gave an equal amount into the insurance scheme, and if the worker became sick or lost his or her job, he or she could claim some benefit. This was the basis of our present National Insurance scheme, and provides us with certain insured benefits.

Insured benefits

Insured benefits are only paid to people who have paid their National Insurance contributions. They include:

Pensions Retirement pensions account for the largest part of the total Social Security budget. The amount of the pension is increased each year to take account of rises in the standard of living. Many people have a firm's pension scheme which they pay into as well, in order to get a larger pension when they retire.

Unemployment benefit Sometimes called the dole, a worker can claim unemployment pay if he loses his job. If he or she was sacked, or left of his or her own accord without good reason, unemployment pay can be withheld for the first six weeks.

Maternity benefits When a woman leaves work to have a baby, she is entitled to maternity pay for the first six weeks of absence. If she has not been working, she will not have paid her National Insurance, and so will not be entitled to the allowance, but she will still be able to claim a maternity grant (currently £25) providing her husband has been paying contributions.

Sick pay If a person is unable to work because of sickness or disability or injury, he or she is entitled to a range of benefits depending on the nature of his or her illness.

Non-insured benefits

There are a number of benefits which are paid anyway, whether or not a person has paid contributions. Most of these depend on a person's income being below a certain level, but one of them, Child Benefit, is payable to everyone who has children, irrespective of income.

Child benefit Used to be called Family Allowance, and is often still known by its old name. Child Benefit is a monthly payment made to the mother (although the father can also cash the cheques) through the Post Office. In cases of hardship, and for people who were receiving it before 1982, it is paid weekly. Family Allowance was first introduced to persuade people to have more children!

Supplementary benefit This is an allowance, or a lump sum, paid to anyone who has not got a job, nor any income, nor any savings. It is not a great deal, and is intended only to provide the basics of food, housing and clothes to people who otherwise would not be able to afford them.

Family income supplement This is an allowance paid to people who are working, but whose income is too low to support their family. Both a person's income, and the size of their family, are taken into account when working out what the allowance will be. It is not possible to claim Supplementary Benefit when you are working, which is why Family Income Supplement was brought in.

Education and health allowances These are slightly different in that they are paid by the Health Service, or local authority's Education

Departments, but they have the same effect of helping less well off families. They include free school meals, uniform allowances, grants for staying on at school, free prescriptions, free dental care, and so on.

How to claim

Information on allowances is available from Citizen's Advice Bureaux, and Health and Social Security buildings. Some people do not like to claim their full allowances, thinking of it as charity, but this is certainly not the case, particularly with the insured benefits, which people claiming have already paid their contributions for.

Statutory and voluntary bodies

As well as money, there is a range of ways in which government helps the less well off members of society. Services provided by the government are known as Statutory Services. Services provided by groups of individuals (and there are hundreds of these) are known as Voluntary Services.

The most obvious Statutory Service is the provision of social workers to help people with their problems, but there are also many other services for the elderly — day centres where they can relax together, Home Helps to clean and tidy for them; for the mentally handicapped — Adult Training Centres where they can do some useful work, homes and hospitals to care for them; and for other disadvantaged groups.

As mentioned above, there are literally hundreds of voluntary helping organizations for people with various problems, ranging from Alcoholics Anonymous, Doctor Barnardo's Homes, the Women's Royal Voluntary Service (providing among other things Meals on Wheels and Hospital Canteens), the Salvation Army, and the Red Cross and St John's Ambulance Brigade, to very specific smaller groups like the Muscular Dystrophy Association.

Something to do . . . .

Visit your local Department of Health and Social Security and look at the range of leaflets they will have covering the allowances they offer. Also go to a centre for Voluntary Services, if you have one, or your Citizen's Advice Bureau, and look at the lists of voluntary organizations they will have. Can you find organizations to help the following:

single parent families
sufferers from cystic fibrosis
gamblers
people who have lost relatives

Do any of your local Churches take part in Voluntary Work? You could ask a local minister or vicar to tell you about this.

Can you help? What part could you play in providing these services?

Inflation and unemployment

The balloon goes up

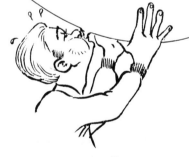

How often have you heard your parents comparing prices today with what they used to be in the past? Or saying how little pocket money they used to be given, and what they could buy with it? This increasing of prices year by year is called <u>inflation,</u> and over your lifetime has been really dramatic. For instance in 1967 a Mars bar cost 2p, as did a bag of crisps. A loaf of bread was under 5p, and for 50p you could buy a gallon of petrol, ten cigarettes, a pint of beer, and still have enough change for fish and chips! Some things have gone up in price more than others. Postage has gone from 1½p to 15½p – a rise of ten times, but records have only gone from 33p to £1.10, a rise of three times. It is possible, however, to take an <u>average</u> of the sort of things people tend to buy — a sort of shopping basket including everything from bread to bus fares — and measure how its <u>total</u> price changes from year to year, or month to month. This total is called the <u>Retail Price Index,</u> or RPI, and is worked out and published each month. Before 1970 prices had always gone up a little from year to year, but it was during the 1970s that the rises started to get really big, and in some years inflation rose to over 20%. Over the decade as a whole the Retail Price Index quadrupled, which means on average prices in 1980 were four times what they were in 1970. Of course wages had gone up a lot too.

Inflation has now dropped to around 10%, but even this means that prices will double in seven years and quadruple in fourteen.

Does inflation matter?

That depends on who you are. If you are working, and your income goes up each year by the same amount as the rise in the RPI, then in one sense inflation will not affect you. However the RPI only takes an average of price rises, and what you yourself choose to buy, or have to buy (like food, housing and fuel) might have gone up by more than the average. Even if you are not working, providing whatever money you do get (like a pension) is 'index-linked' (that means it goes up each year by exactly the same amount as the RPI) you may not be unduly affected. But if your

187

income does not rise as much as prices, or if your pension is not index-linked, you will fairly quickly suffer through inflation. And the higher inflation is, the more people there are who are likely to be in that position, and the more they will suffer.

Another problem with inflation is its effect on industry. Unless a firm constantly puts up its prices (which may stop it selling its goods), it will soon find that its raw materials cost more than the money it has been getting for its finished products. If this happens it will not make any profit and may go bankrupt. Also planning ahead is very difficult if you have no idea how much prices or wages will rise.

The inflationary spiral

Inflation tends to feed on itself, and spiral upwards. People do not want to save, because they see the value of their savings slipping away. And they want to borrow, because the money they pay back is worth less than what they borrowed. Therefore the higher inflation is, the more they spend, which pushes inflation still higher. The classic case of inflation getting completely out of control happened in Germany between the World Wars, when even postage stamps ended up costing millions of pfennigs, and people rushed out to spend all their pay as soon as they got it, before prices rose again.

Causes of inflation

The wealth of a country, as you know, is measured by the amount of goods and services produced in that country. If the amount of money in circulation (called the *money supply*) goes up without the wealth of the country increasing (which happens if people borrow more) then everything will cost more, since there is more money to share between the same amount of goods. This is called **demand** inflation.

Alternatively, if a firm pays its workers higher wages and gets the money to do so by putting up its prices rather than by increasing productivity or improving efficiency, providing people will still buy its goods this too will cause inflation. This is called **cost** inflation.

The cure?

The cure is to increase output to match any increase in the money supply, or to prevent people getting hold of the money to pay higher prices. The problem is how to do this. The government does not have complete control over the economy, and even if it did, could never be quite sure of what effect its controls were going to have. Put simply, will increasing the tax on beer raise more money for the government, or merely stop people drinking beer?

The Conservative Government elected in 1979 has tried to reduce inflation by controlling the money supply and increasing output. They have not been altogether very successful. They have certainly cut down the amount of money people have been able to spend, and this has probably kept inflation lower than it would otherwise have been. And during the same time they have caused productivity to rise − each worker is now producing more than before. But, as we saw earlier an enormous amount of spending and borrowing is done by the government itself, and strangely enough the government has been less successful in controlling this. And although each worker is producing more than previously, because there are fewer people at work, *total* production is still lower than in 1979.

Many people now think the government is trying to solve the wrong problem. It is not inflation, but unemployment that is our biggest economic worry. The government say (rightly) that the rise in unemployment is not entirely their fault, and (perhaps rightly, but perhaps not) that now industry is more efficient unemployment will soon start to fall.

Prime Minister Margaret Thatcher

Unemployment

People go to work for a lot of reasons, not all of them to do with money. They want to spend their time in a useful and constructive way; they want to help the community; and they want to exercise their skills and abilities. Some people do these things without getting paid — mothers bringing up their children, people doing voluntary work, or people engaging in their hobbies. Do you think Sir Edmund Hillary climbed Mount Everest because he was paid to be an explorer?

On the other hand, everyone wants to share in the wealth of our society, and at the moment, unless you are too old or too young to work, this usually means having a job to provide the money for you and your family to buy the things you want and need.

Ideally, there should be a job available for everyone who wants one. This does not mean everyone will always be at work. Some people will choose not to work, and others will be temporarily unemployed while they are 'between jobs'. In the first case the numbers are usually very small, and 'Employment Exchanges' (now Jobcentres) were set up in 1910 to help those in the second category.

Between 1945 and 1970 this accounted for practically everyone who was unemployed (about half a million people) — there were effectively jobs for everyone. However since 1970 unemployment has risen well beyond this level, and there are now more people unemployed in Britain (some 3 million) than ever before, most of whom want very much to work, but cannot find jobs.

Causes and cures

The cause of present unemployment is partly a decline in traditional industries, and partly cheap competition from abroad, but mainly a general low level of demand for goods and services in the country, and indeed the world, as a whole. The decline started in 1973 when the price of

190

imported oil increased dramatically. In the past, governments have over-come such low demand by increasing their own spending, and encouraging other people to increase theirs, to build up demand for goods. However as we have seen, when this was tried in the 1970s it only led to high inflation, and the government does not want to make the same mistake again.

An alternative is to increase demand by making goods *cheaper*. This can be done by increasing productivity so that each worker makes more goods. In the short term this does not help unemployment – quite the opposite – but it might do eventually. During the Industrial Revolution the new machines led to a lot of people being made *redundant* (no longer needed by a particular factory), but enormously increased employment as a whole both by increasing the demand for the new, cheaper goods, and by increasing the wealth of the country which caused a rise in employment in other spheres. In general, increased automation leads to fewer jobs in the factory concerned at the time, but more jobs eventually, both in factories and, more especially, in service industries.

Questions

1 What is inflation?

2 Why is it not a good idea to save money in a teapot under your bed?

3 Can you name *three* jobs which people do without getting paid?

4 What does it mean if someone is 'between jobs'?

5 Why does the government not reduce unemployment by encouraging people to spend more money to buy more goods?

6 Why does inflation 'feed on itself' to produce still higher inflation?

7 Do you think it is worth putting up with higher inflation if this means lower unemployment? Say why, or why not.

8 What is index-linking? See if you can find examples of payments or interest rates which are index-linked.

And what about the future?

Chips with everything!
Billy: 'What's for lunch today?'
Susan: 'Fish fingers and chips.'
Billy: 'I like chips with everything!'

No, we are not going to talk about chips made from potatoes, you can see your Home Economics teacher to find out how to do that! We are going to talk about chips made from silicon – silicon chips.

Billy: 'What's silicon?'

Susan:	'After oxygen, the most common element on earth. All sand, all soil, and most rocks contain silicon. Altogether, a quarter of the earth's crust is silicon.'
Billy:	'So what's a silicon chip?'
Susan:	'I haven't the remotest idea, but I know there's one in my digital watch, and one in your calculator.'

The new technology

Technology is using inventions and machines to help improve production. As we have seen, there was an enormous advance in technology during the Industrial Revolution with the invention and use of the steam engine, metal machinery, and the power and heat from coal and gas. Since then, technology has continued to advance, but more slowly, with the development of the internal combustion engine, the aeroplane, and electricity. However we are now in the middle, or perhaps at the beginning, of another very rapid period of advancement with the development of technology based on the *silicon chip*. This silicon chip technology is sometimes referred to as the *new technology*, and is beginning to have a big effect on how we live and work.

'So what's a silicon chip?'

When computers were first built in the late 1940s, they used thousands of *valves* all joined with wires. A valve looks a bit like a thin light bulb, and these early computers were very large and very expensive. They could do a lot of calculations very quickly, however, and could store and manipulate huge quantities of information. So the search was on to make them smaller and cheaper. This was partly achieved by the invention of the *transistor*, which does much the same as a valve, but is much smaller, is not made of glass, and uses less electricity. Transistors enabled small battery powered radios to be made for the first time.

Radio valves

192

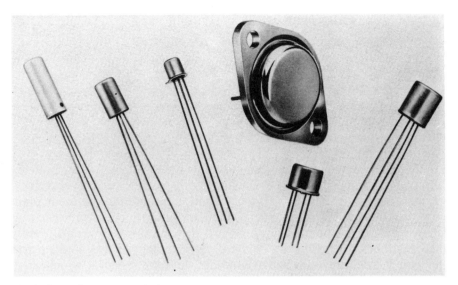

Typical transistor encapsulations

The real breakthrough came, however, when it was discovered that not only transistors, but also whole circuits of wires could be 'printed' ('etched' is a closer description of the process) onto wafer-thin slices of silicon. These slices of silicon, with their printed circuits and connectors are the so called 'silicon chips', sometimes called 'microprocessers'.

Nowadays, tens of thousands of transistors and related circuitry can be printed on to a slice of silicon the size of your thumbnail. Not only are these micro-processors much smaller than previous computers, they are also much, much cheaper. Although the printing is very complicated and relies upon, amongst other things, the bombarding of the slice of silicon

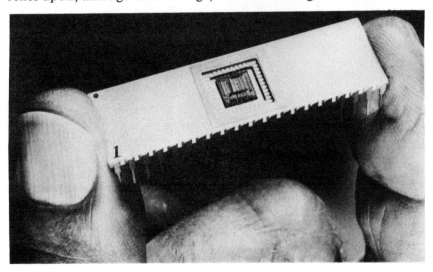

The Ferranti F100-L microprocessor

with atomic particles, chips can be mass produced in great numbers, and the basic raw material – silicon – is very common, and therefore cheap.

You can now hold in your hand the processing unit for a computer which fifteen years ago would have taken up a whole room and cost literally hundreds of thousands of pounds.

What do they do?

1 Control machinery

Think of a chip as a collection of switches which can be turned on and off in any order thousands of times per second, in accordance with any plan you care to give it. This plan can either be built into the chip, or fed in later while you are operating it, and is called the chip's *program*. Using these switches, the chip can *control* any machinery it is wired up to. Because of the huge number of switches, and the speed at which they

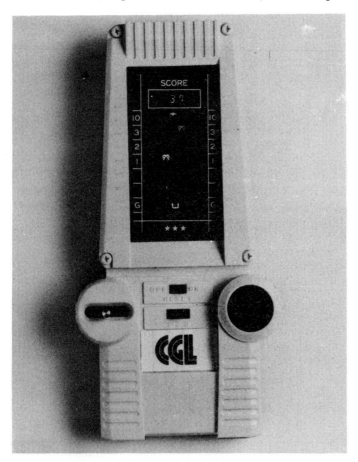

The Galaxy Invader, Computer Games Ltd

work, a chip can control much more complicated machinery much more accurately than a human operator could.

Example . . . .

When playing a 'space invaders' machine you press the 'fire' button. The machine's micro-processor, or chip, then operates all the appropriate lights, sounds and scoring devices in the right order. It is controlling all the parts of the machine in a pre-determined manner, relating to what the machine was showing when you pressed the button. Not only is it more complicated than the old 'pin-ball' machines, but it can be held in your hand! (Try putting a 'pin-ball' machine in your pocket!)

2   Store information

There are many millions of different positions for the switches in a chip, and each position can be made to stand for a particular letter or number. So chips can 'remember' pieces of information, and can then sort, store or compare them.

What use are they?

They are incredibly useful. Every machine which needs controlling can be controlled more accurately with a microprocessor. Among existing machines which have been adapted to 'chip control' are deep freezers, ovens, washing machines, sewing machines, cash registers, packing machines, central heating systems, car ignition systems and televisions.

But much more important is their use in machines which were too complicated to work at all without the chip's ability to control or remember, and could not be made small or cheap enough using old-style computers.

We describe a few 'new technology' inventions of the 1970's below.

Calculators

Among the first of the new inventions, we hardly need to mention the effect calculators have had. And remember that in 1970 *they did not exist*.

Word processors

A word processor is a bit like a typewriter, only when the operator types, the letters come up in a row of lights, and are then transferred to paper using ink jets at incredible speed. Whole sentences or even pages can be remembered by the machine and typed at the press of one key. Part of a letter can be typed automatically, and then the machine will stop for a single word, perhaps a person's name, to be inserted by the operator to make the letter look personal. One machine can do the work of a whole team of typists.

The Hewlett-Packard 38C calculator

Robots

One of the most important new inventions is the industrial robot. Forget about eight foot high metal men with ray guns and electronic voices –

The robot weld body production, British Leyland, Longbridge

industrial robots are built to do one job only, and look rather like boxes with one long arm. The arm can be controlled (by the microprocessor) to move to any position and then lift something, move it, or work a hand-held machine, like a spot-welder, a paint spray, a glass cutter, or a drill. The majority of robots work to an accuracy of 1 mm, but they can be made even more precise.

'Talking' machines

The most recent inventions use the chip to control 'voice synthesizers' which mimic the human voice and can talk to you. One such device can read print with a camera and convert it to speech. (To help blind people for example.) Others can be linked to telephones in booking offices, or even translating machines. The days of being able to talk into a microphone in English, and having your words come out of a speaker in, say, French, are not far off.

The IBM 'Talking Terminal'

Digital watches

The timer is a quartz crystal rather than a balance wheel, and control is by a chip. Unlike old style watches there are no moving parts and so accuracy up to 5 seconds a month can be achieved. The most expensive jewelled lever watches can get nowhere near this accuracy.

197

Seiko Time (UK) Ltd

Toys and games

These break down into three groups: calculator-type games, like spelling or arithmetic games; video or TV games; and model games, like controlling a model car with a hand held ultra sonic device. All share the requirement of a chip to control their many functions. In fact before the invention of the chip, the electronics needed to control the model car would hardly have fitted into a double decker bus!

Speak and Spell, Texas Instruments

THINK

When Neil Armstrong stepped on the moon in 1969, he would not have understood the technology behind a digital watch — they had not yet been invented.

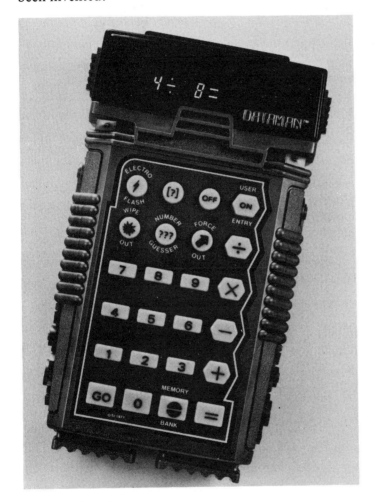

Dataman, Texas Instruments

Suggested work

1   What is a silicon chip?

2   What *two* things can a silicon chip do?

3 What advantages do industrial robots have over human workers?

4 Is the development of the new technology likely to lead to more people being employed in manufacturing industry, or less?
  Give examples of the types of job which could be replaced by microprocessors or robots, and those extra jobs which microprocessors will bring.

5 Choose the *three* inventions based on the silicon chip we have described which you think are the biggest advances. Describe them and say why you picked them.

6 What things do you have at home controlled by silicon chips?

7 '*Journey into the future*'. Imagine you are living in Britain in the year 2025. You can either be yourself at the age you will be then, or a young person just leaving school. Describe what you think your home and job will be like then. Start like this: 'I stretched lazily as the alarm sounded . . . .'

Sample multiple choice questions

1 Mr and Mrs Dhillon have four children. Although Mr Dhillon works, he only earns a small wage and the family are having difficulty making ends meet. The family should apply for
  a) supplementary benefit
  b) needs allowance
  c) family income supplement
  d) unemployment benefit

2 In order to vote in a general election a person must be
  a) over 21
  b) a householder
  c) of British birth and nationality
  d) on the electoral roll

3 Which of the following is a local authority responsibility?
  a) defence
  b) education
  c) social security
  d) foreign affairs

4 'Gross' pay means
  a) pay before deductions
  b) pay after deductions
  c) pay after National Insurance
  d) a firm's total wage bill

5 A rates rebate is a
  a) refund of some of the payable rates
  b) claim for exemption from tax

c) measure of the rentable value of a house

d) payment from the government to local authorities

6   Which of the following benefits depends on the claimant having paid National Insurance contributions?
a) unemployment pay
b) child benefit
c) supplementary benefit
d) family income supplement

7   The Chairman of the House of Commons is called the
a) Sergeant at Arms
b) Chancellor of the Exchequer
c) Speaker
d) Cabinet

8   A by-election might be held
a) because the government had resigned
b) because the government had held office for five years
c) because the people wanted a change of MP
d) because the sitting MP had died

9   The Meals on Wheels service is run by the
a) local authority
b) WRVS
c) social services department
d) Red Cross

10   The area represented by a Member of Parliament is called a
a) boundary
b) ward
c) division
d) constituency

11   The process of prices increasing year by year is called
a) inflation
b) deflation
c) monetarism
d) demarcation

12   Which of the following machines could have been invented without the silicon chip?
a) word processer
b) digital watch
c) colour television
d) industrial robot

13   Which of these materials is the most common?
a) silicon
b) iron
c) krypton

Sociology Dept. Univ. of London Goldsmiths' College New Cross, SE14 6NW

d) coal

14 Which of the following has not led to an increase in unemployment?
a) the decline of old industries
b) increased competition from abroad
c) an increasing number of bankruptcies
d) increased profitability

15 Who commands the Armed Services?
a) the Prime Minister
b) the Queen
c) the House of Commons
d) the House of Lords

Index